D0114142

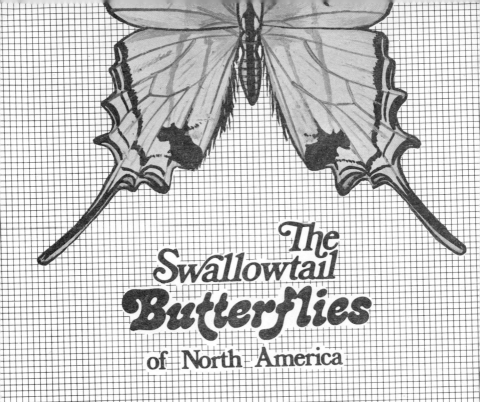

The Swallowtail Butterflies
of North America

Hamilton A. Tyler

color plates by **Donald Phillips**
line drawings by **Gary Lisandrelli**

NATUREGRAPH PUBLISHERS

Library of Congress Cataloging in Publication Data
Tyler, Hamilton A
    The swallowtail butterflies of North America

    Bibliography: p.
    Includes indexes.
    1. Papilionidae—Identification.. 2. Butter-
flies—North America—Identification.   I. Title.
QL561.P2T8   595.7'89   75-30569

Second Printing with Revisions

All Rights Reserved

Printed in U. S. A.

ISBN 0-87961-039-5 Cloth Edition
ISBN 0-87961-038-7 Paper Edition

Published by Naturegraph Publishers, Inc., Healdsburg, Ca. 95448

CONTENTS

COMMON NAMES OF SPECIES IN THIS BOOK

LIST OF SPECIES

Chapter 3
Papilio

1. *machaon*, Pl. I, Fig. 1,2,3
2. *polyxenes*, Pl. I, Fig. 4,5,6,7
3. *kahli*, no Fig.
4. *brevicauda*, Pl. III, Fig. 1
5. *bairdii*, Pl. II, Fig. 1,2,3
6. *oregonius*, Pl. II, Fig. 5
7. *joanae*, no Fig.
8. *zelicaon*, Pl. II, Fig. 4
9. *nitra*, Pl. III, Fig. 2
10. *rudkini*, Pl. II, Fig. 6
11. *indra*, Pl. III, Fig. 3,4,5,6

Chapter 5
Papilio

12. *glaucus*, Pl. IV, Fig. 1,2,5,7,8
13. *rutulus*, Pl. IV, Fig. 3,4
14. *alexiares*, Pl. V, Fig. 6
15. *eurymedon*, Pl. V, Fig. 1
16. *multicaudatus*, Pl. IV, Fig. 6
17. *pilumnus*, Pl. V, Fig. 2
18. *troilus*, Pl. V, Fig. 3,4
19. *palamedes*, Pl. V, Fig. 5

Chapter 6
Papilio

20. *cresphontes*, Pl. VI, Fig. 1
21. *thoas*, Pl. VI, Fig. 2
22. *ornythion*, Pl. VII, Fig. 5,6
23. *astyalus*, Pl. VI, Fig. 5,6
24. *androgeus*, Pl. VII, Fig. 1,2,4
25. *aristodemus*, Pl. VI, Fig. 3
26. *andraemon*, Pl. VII, Fig. 3

Chapter 8
Papilio

27. *anchisiades*, Pl. VIII, Fig. 1,2
28. *pharnaces*, Pl. VIII, Fig. 4
29. *erostratus*, Pl. VIII, Fig. 5,6
30. *erostratinus*, Pl. VIII, Fig. 7,8
31. *rogeri*, Pl. VIII, Fig. 3
32. *torquatus*, Pl. IX, Fig. 1,2
33. *victorinus*, Pl. IX, Fig. 3,4
34. *diazi*, Pl. VI, Fig. 4
35. *garamas*, Pl. IX, Fig. 5
36. *abderus*, Pl. IX, Fig. 6

Chapter 9
Eurytides

37. *marcellus*, Pl. X, Fig. 1,2,3,4
38. *philolaus*, Pl. X, Fig. 5,6
39. *oberthueri*, Pl. XII, Fig. 1
40. *epidaus*, Pl. XII, Fig. 4,6
41. *branchus*, Pl. XI, Fig. 6
42. *belesis*, Pl. XI, Fig. 3
43. *thymbraeus*, Pl. XI, Fig. 1,2
44. *phaon*, Pl. XI, Fig. 4,5
45. *agesilaus*, Pl. XII, Fig. 2,3
46. *protesilaus*, Pl. XII, Fig. 5
47. *marchandi*, Pl. XIII, Fig. 1
48. *lacandones*, Pl. XIII, Fig. 3
49. *calliste*, Pl. XIII, Fig. 2
50. *salvini*, Pl. XIII, Fig. 4

Chapter 11
Parides

51. *photinus*, Pl. XIV, Fig. 1
52. *alopius*, Pl. XIII, Fig. 5
53. *montezuma*, Pl. XIV, Fig. 2
54. *sesostris*, Pl. XIII, Fig. 6
55. *polyzelus*, Pl. XIV, Fig. 3
56. *iphidamas*, Pl. XIV, Fig. 5,6
57. *arcas*, Pl. XIV, Fig. 4

Battus

58. *philenor*, Pl. XV, Fig. 1
59. *polydamas*, Pl. XV, Fig. 2
60. *eracon*, Pl. XV, Fig. 3
61. *belus*, Pl. XV, Fig. 4
62. *laodamas*, Pl. XV, Fig. 5
63. *lycidas*, Pl. XV, Fig. 6

Chapter 12
Parnassius

64. *eversmanni*, Pl. XVI, Fig. 1,2
65. *clodius*, Pl. XVI, Fig. 5,6
66. *phoebus*, Pl. XVI, Fig. 3,4

Chapter 13
Baronia

67. *brevicornis*, Pl. XVI, Fig. 7,8

LINE DRAWINGS

MAPS

ABBREVIATIONS

c., e., n., s., w.: central, eastern, northern, etc.

Co., Cos., co., cos.: County, Counties, county, counties.

E, N, S, W: east, north, south, west.

ec., ne., sw.: east-central, northeastern, southwestern, etc.

f.: form.

m: meter(s) *mm*: millimeter(s).

mts.: mountains.

prov.: province (of Canada).

sp.: species.

submarg.: submarginal.

subsp.: subspecies.

Swt.: Swallowtail.

UpFW: upper surface of forewing.

UnFW: under surface of forewing.

UpHW: upper surface of hind wing.

UnHW: under surface of hind wing.

♂: male (♂♂: plural).

♀: female (♀♀: plural).

ACKNOWLEDGMENTS

One of the many pleasant aspects of the study of butterflies is the ready help offered by fellow lepidopterists and biologists. I am grateful to the following for answering questions and supplying information: John R. Arnold, F. Martin Brown, John T. Cooper, John De Benedictis, Alberto Diaz Frances, John F. Emmel, Dr. Tarsicio Escalante, Michael Fisher, Marc Grinnell, Frank R. Hedges, Steven Kohler, John A. Legge Jr., Timothy McCabe, James R. Mori, Fred T. Naumann, James Oberfoell, Prof. R.L. Post, Dr. Tommaso Racheli, Eduardo C. Welling, and Robert Wind. In addition, Prof. John Arnold read all and Michael Fisher read parts of a first draft of the manuscript, and both offered valuable suggestions. Prof. Arthur M. Shapiro and Steven R. Sims read a second version, and a number of their observations have been incorporated, adding much of value to the text. Since the use made of the information offered by those listed above was not in their hands, none is responsible for errors occurring in the presentation. Finally I should like to thank Brooking Tatum, who in many important respects was a colleague as well as the editor and contributed much to both the shape and the content of this book.

The author would like to receive both corrections of and additions to this account of North American Swallowtails, particularly further information on distribution and habitats. After a time has passed the author will distribute a sheet of the more important emendations to anyone requesting it.

Address:

Hamilton Tyler
8450 West Dry Creek Road
Healdsburg, California 95448

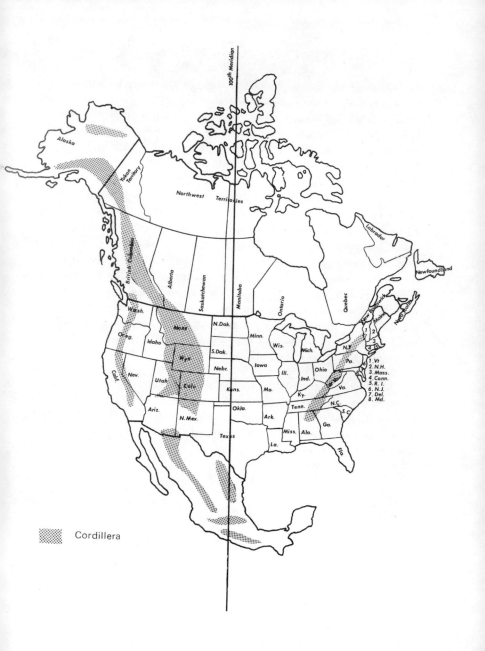

Map 1. Cordilleras (mountain chains) of North America, with political divisions of U.S. and Canada.

1

INTRODUCTION

Almost everyone can correctly point out a Swallowtail butterfly, and those who know their local trees, birds and wildflowers are likely to call several Swallowtails by name, since every continental state has from two to a dozen species of these large and conspicuous butterflies. For the person with a general curiosity about wildlife this book is intended as a guide in finding local species of Swallowtails or, when traveling farther afield, for identifying the unfamiliar species. For one who ventures far, or thinks of doing so, all of North America is here included from the arctic coast of Alaska to the southern boundary of Mexico. Taken together, this survey gives some account of how the Swallowtail Family of butterflies adapts to all of the habitats of North America: to arctic tundra, to coniferous forests including mountains of 13,000 feet or more, to deciduous woodlands, to desert and plateau areas, to tropical rain forests, or to plowed fields and city gardens; all of these habitats have their Swallowtails.

If, within that vast region, one finds an unknown Swallowtail, this book should prove helpful in determining first its name and then something of its relationship to other members of the family. The best procedure may be to consult the plates first, as there will be at least one named figure resembling the specimen in hand or the individual seen. Next one should locate that name in the text, where the distinguishing characteristics of similar species, subspecies or forms are given. An important point to observe is that a fragile butterfly often loses many of its scales. Any specimen which can be picked up easily will be in poor condition, with changed colors and perhaps altered pattern. If the specimen in hand fits both plate and text, consider the distribution of the species. Butterflies sometimes stray or are windblown for a distance, but not nearly so far nor so often as is true of birds. One is unlikely to find a butterfly far outside its known range. If the stated distribution embraces the point of observation or collection, and the specimen agrees with both description and figure, one should have little doubt about naming the particular Swallowtail.

Some of these brightly colored butterflies attracted attention long before the facts about insects were collected into what is now the science of entomology, and North American Swallowtails were among the first to be illustrated in books. In 1587 John White brought to England a colored painting of the Eastern Tiger Swallowtail, *Papilio glaucus*, a species he had seen in the colony of Virginia. His drawing was published as a black-and-white woodcut in 1634.

Knowledge of North American Swallowtails continued well ahead of information on those in some other parts of the world. Our Zebra Swallowtail, *Eurytides marcellus*, was described by Petiver in 1699. Interest in natural history increased tremendously during the 18th century, leading to the publication in 1758 of the tenth edition of Linnaeus's *System of Nature*, which is the foundation of the present system for classifying both plants and animals. In that and the subsequent editions the Swallowtails, with brief descriptions and Latin names, have a prime place among the butterflies. Some of the generic and specific names have changed since then but the system has held.

The scientific study of Lepidoptera, as moths, skippers and butterflies are collectively called, had an important American inception. An English artist-naturalist, John Abbot, traveled to Virginia in 1773, and then on to Georgia. He made hundreds of drawings of insects and birds, some of which were published in book form by James Edward Smith as *The Rarer Lepidopterous Insects of Georgia* in 1797. Pictured in the book are the Pipevine Swallowtail, the Black Swallowtail, the Zebra Swallowtail, and the *ilioneus* subspecies of the Spicebush Swallowtail. The remarkable thing about Abbot's work is that his illustrations include the larvae and pupae, along with an account of the life history and the larval food plants used by each species.

2

Other early illustrations of American Swallowtails occur in an incomplete project called, *Peale's Lepidoptera Americana*, printed in Philadelphia in 1833. On the first plate, uncolored, are figures of the Pale Swallowtail, now *Papilio eurymedon*, and the Two-tailed Swallowtail, *Papilio multicaudatus*. Surprisingly these are both *western* species, but the familiar Eastern Tiger Swallowtail was also shown on a setting board to indicate the technique of mounting these insects.

We have begun this account with the names of a few individual species, which is somewhat the way the scientific study of Lepidoptera began—by collecting and naming individual kinds, and then gathering these into closely related groups called families, one of which is the family Papilionidae, or Swallowtails and relatives. A family is further subdivided into genera, and each genus comprises a group of species more closely related to each other than to members of other genera. In this book the classification of Munroe, now used by the British Museum (Natural History), is followed, dividing North American members of the family into the following genera: *Papilio, Eurytides, Parides, Battus, Parnassius,* and *Baronia*. In terms of evolution the first named is presumably the most recent, and the last the most ancient, but the sequence is not lineal so the first three genera may be of more or less the same age.

The family belongs to a larger unit, the order, and in this case it is the order Lepidoptera, or scale-winged insects. The insect world is divided into more than two dozen such orders, but only the Lepidoptera concern us. Insects of this order have veined, membranous wings which are in most species covered with minute scales. These scales, together with the veins, are responsible for the divers patterns displayed. In the following pages Swallowtails will be identified whenever possible by the wing patterns, since these can be seen with the naked eye.

With few exceptions, moths can be distinguished from butterflies by their nocturnal habits. Anatomically, moths have a structural array (the *frenulum*) (or *jugum*, in some primitive forms) for locking the fore and hind wings together in flight. Butterflies have only an expanded surface (humeral lobe) on the hind wing to provide an underlap and keep wings united. Also, moths lack the clubbed antennae found on butterflies. In terms of number there may be as many as 112,000 species in the order Lepidoptera, and there is general agreement that the butterflies number about 13,000 species. In the sequence of evolution, many authorities believe, moths were the first members of the order to appear, followed by skippers, and then the true butterflies. It is interesting to note that most serious students feel that Swallowtails of the family Papilionidae were the first true butterflies to evolve, followed by the Sulphurs and Whites of the family Pieridae, then by other families of butterflies. There is no way to determine the number of extinct Swallowtails but the surviving species number somewhere around 550, making it a small though diverse family. This book describes 67 presumed species, of which a half dozen or more may lose that rank upon further study of their genetic make-up, and these will then be classed as subspecies or forms. The doubtful ones are indicated in the text.

LIFE HISTORY

When the weather is fine in a garden or when we take spring and summer walks in the countryside, butterflies always seem to be there, so we think of them as a fixed part of the environment. In actual fact butterflies are much like summer annuals among flowers, and most of them have a shorter 'blooming' period. A few, notably the Monarch and members of the Tortoise-Shell group, hibernate through the winter and lay eggs the following spring, but for most kinds the adult life span may be only one or two weeks, or barely the time necessary for mating and depositing eggs for the next generation. Life-span studies in Trinidad show that even in that seasonless climate Swallowtails have an average life span of five to ten days. However, studies in Costa Rica indicate that individuals there may live as long as four or five months. In northern latitudes the second or third brood, when present, has a very short time indeed before the frosts come and the season ends.

Since the butterflies do survive from year to year it is evident that the adult life span is only a small part of the cycle; even though most of this book is concerned with the adult stage, some account should be taken of the early stages. Members of the order Lepidoptera undergo a complete metamorphosis: from the egg hatches a caterpillar which sheds its skin before each stage of growth, turns into a pupa or chrysalis, and finally emerges as the adult butterfly or moth. One can make some generalizations about these stages within the True Swallowtails. Their eggs, with two exceptions in our area, are spherical but flattened slightly where fixed to plant leaf or stem (Fig. 1-1). The initial color is usually cream or greenish, but as incubation proceeds the egg darkens, even to black at the time of hatching. A few species are colonial, in the narrow sense of being gregarious in the caterpillar stage, and the eggs of these are laid in groups; but for most species the eggs are laid singly and usually some distance apart. Generally, one specific kind of food plant is selected but eggs will be deposited on a number of different individual plants of that species.

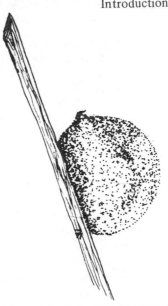

Figure 1-1. Egg of *Papilio oregonius* (after Perkins et al.).

In temperate regions emergence from the pupal state of suspended animation (diapause) is initiated by the warm temperatures of spring, following the winter period of chilling. In the arid tropics emergence seems to be influenced by moisture, which is opportune since the butterfly then emerges to lay its eggs when the same moisture has awakened tender growth in the food plant. Even where the climate varies little in temperature a rhythm remains for individual species so that they may emerge at different times. Under optimal conditions an egg may hatch in six or seven days, but the period can be as short as four days, or very much longer if weather is unfavorable.

Emergence of the adults is often divided, with the males coming out first so that they will be dried, exercised, and in full potency to greet the emerging female. After she has mated (copulated) fertilization takes some time, varying from a few hours to a day or more; the sperm remain alive so that an entire batch of eggs can be fertilized from one mating. In copulation the sperm are deposited in a neat capsule (spermatophore), and more than one male may mate with the same female.

The newly hatched caterpillar is very small, perhaps 3 mm long, and unlike its adult parents it is equipped with chewing mouthparts. Its first meal is likely to be the remainder of the egg, then the preferred leaves or flowers. As growth is extremely rapid the caterpillar must shed its skin from time to time to allow for expansion, and the periods between moults are called instars, or more simply, stages. Commonly there are five of these stages, but six and even seven also occur. The first and crucial stage often begins with some hesitation about eating, and it takes the right kind of leaf in a tender phase of growth to induce feeding. Many newly hatched caterpillars die at this juncture. Once begun, feeding is vigorous for a while, and is then followed by complete rest until another burst of feeding begins.

At the end of any stage the caterpillar goes into a state of torpor. The moult which follows seems to require an extra effort, as the larva is more likely to die at that juncture than while feeding. There are changes in appearance between the various stages and markedly between the first and the final (mature) stage (Figure 1-2, a, b, c). For example the larvae of the Anise and Indra Swallowtails look alike in the first stage, being spiny, black and marked in the middle with a white saddle. By the second stage the Anise has developed orange spots at the base of its tubercles, while Indra remains black and white. In its final stage the Indra has pink transverse bands with yellow dots, contrasting with a smooth, black body, while the Anise has a green body banded with black, and the spines have become flat, rounded, orange spots. The final stage lasts longer than the early ones, taking perhaps nine days instead of five.

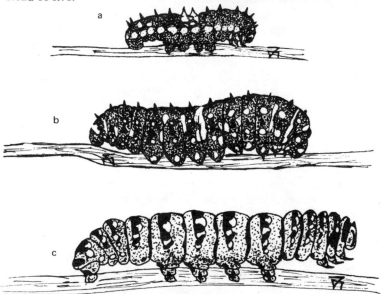

Figure 1-2. Caterpillar of Anise Swallowtail (*P. zelicaon*). *a.* Second stage. *b.* Fourth stage. *c.* Final stage.

6

As the final stage draws to a close the caterpillar becomes restive, and then searches out a suitable place for pupation. The True Swallowtails pupate in an upright position, secured to a suitable vertical surface. First a silken pad is spun upon the chosen surface by a spinneret on the lower lip. The posterior end of the abdomen is then attached to that base by hooks (the cremaster). Next a silken sling (girdle) is spun around the middle of the body and secured to the surface, to hold it upright. Finally, the last larval skin is shed, revealing a green or brown chrysalis (pupa) curving outward and upward from the stem or limb like a stub branch (Fig. 1-3).

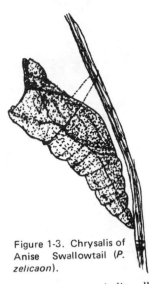

Figure 1-3. Chrysalis of Anise Swallowtail (*P. zelicaon*).

Within the pupal case the caterpillar's inner structure is literally dissolved, and the cells are rearranged in the configuration of the adult butterfly. These transformations may be quite rapid, as an adult of a second brood can emerge in as little as nine days after pupation. Where there is but one brood a year, the pupal contents may remain a mass of undifferentiated cells from the time of pupation in June until mid-September, at which time the adult form begins to take shape, a process which may not be completed until midwinter. Times noted for the duration of the pupal stage are thirteen days for the Idaeus Swallowtail, seventeen for the Red and Blue Cattle Heart, ten days for the Thoas Swallowtail, nine for the western subspecies of the Epidaus Swallowtail, and two hundred and one days for its eastern race—the extended time here resulting from overwintering.

The time of emergence is not as simply determined as responding to the first breath of spring, for there are several timing mechanisms in play which relate to temperature, interacting with day length and moisture. Some Spicebush and Pipevine Swallowtails responding to favorable weather will emerge as early as late January in southern Georgia, but for the most part emergence is not sporadic across the months but rather is accomplished in discrete broods of highly determined duration. A brood will encompass four to five weeks, and even in difficult environments like the Rockies, where cold snaps and sudden snow flurries may occur during a spring emergence, the span of a month or so will ensure the survival of at least part of the brood. There is a second survival stratagem which is very important in single-brooded species which inhabit mountain or desert regions, although it is common to all butterflies. When the favorable season arrives some individuals belonging to the brood undergo what is called "standing over," to the following year. The pupa is by far the most durable state of the insect since it can withstand freezing, drought or hurricane, and it has no dependence on a seasonal food plant. Those individuals which stand over, sometimes for as much as six years, protect the species from elimination by a single bad year, and the device likewise makes it possible for a species to extend its range into unfavorable and chancy areas.

A day or two before the adult butterfly is going to emerge its wings become visible through the pupal walls. When the pupal case slowly splits open, a very wet and limp-winged insect struggles out into the world and toward the light; but however wet it may be the addition of wings to the formerly crawling being is most striking. These wings are of double ply, composed of twin parallel membranes which have been folded in the pupa much as a parachute is packed, and the two layers are linked together by strands which will draw them up as the wings are extended. Extension results when the butterfly's vital fluid is pumped between the membranes. The two surfaces are drawn together into contact, and once extended they are supported by hollow veins which become stiff and provide structural rigidity.

Very often butterflies will emerge during the morning hours when increasing light and warmth from the sun will assist in drying their wings. When these are first released they are allowed to hang downward for a preliminary airing, then the wings are flexed slowly while the insect crawls about, until ultimately they can be spread out against the sun's rays. Butterflies are very much children of the sun and its warmth, as they have no heat within to warm their bodies and must depend entirely on that provided by their ambience at any given time. At dawn they may be stiff with cold or even frost, but as the day advances they absorb the sun's heat which gives Swallowtails supplemental energy for their elegant, soaring flights.

BIOGEOGRAPHY

Any species of plant or animal is limited in its distribution by factors such as climate, physical barriers, type of habitat to which it is adapted, the competition of similar species, predation, and, in the case of herbivores such as butterflies in the larval stage, by the distribution of actual and potential food plants. Species of butterflies vary in their ability to tolerate wide environmental differences. The Black Swallowtail is comfortable over much of North America and extends its range into western South America, while its close relative the Short-tailed Swallowtail is entirely restricted to a maritime habitat along the southeastern coast of Canada.

It would be worthwhile to chart the types of habitats and the relationship of each Swallowtail species to them, but there is no room for that project here. Instead, the distribution for each species is noted as carefully as possible, along with a brief comment on habitat preferences. It is hoped that the reader can combine that information with some knowledge of at least United States geography. Map 1 illustrates the political divisions of the United States and Canada, and the major cordilleras of North America. As a generality it may be noted that there are two sets of divisions for the United States and Canada: latitudinal, and longitudinal. There is a northern coniferous forest area with no exact southern border; in the eastern third of the U.S. is a temperate deciduous forest area, or its remnants; and in the extreme south there are subtropical areas. One might think of the Old-World Swallowtail as an inhabitant of coniferous forest, and even tundra, several of the most common eastern Swallowtails as typical of the eastern deciduous forest, and the Palamedes Swallowtail as typical of the se. evergreen forest. The East/West division is even sharper, with distinct sets of species, attributable in part to the effects of glacial ages and, more distantly, to the fact that the West had early links to Asia.

Mexico will be less familiar to most readers, so its place needs a brief comment. The temperate Mexican Plateau stretches from the border of the U.S. deep into Mexico, and although the altitude increases as one proceeds southward the area is in every way a continuation of the North American biological region. There is next a rather abrupt division between this area and the tropics south of it. The dividing line runs along *"la gran sierra volcanica transversal"* (see Maps 2 and 3) from Orizaba in the east to the state of Colima on the West. However, the barrier stops short of the two coastal lowlands, and elements of the tropical fauna make end runs around the barrier along both coasts, reaching to about the Tropic of Cancer, in two narrow bands between the Sierras and the seas.

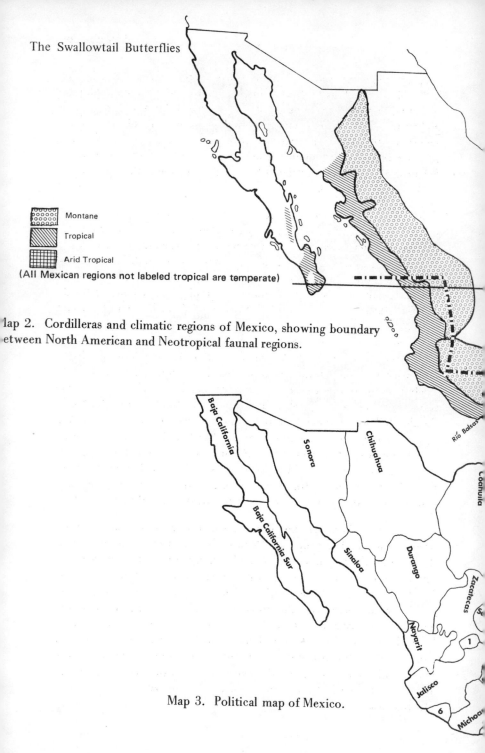

The Swallowtail Butterflies

Montane

Tropical

Arid Tropical

(All Mexican regions not labeled tropical are temperate)

Map 2. Cordilleras and climatic regions of Mexico, showing boundary between North American and Neotropical faunal regions.

Map 3. Political map of Mexico.

10

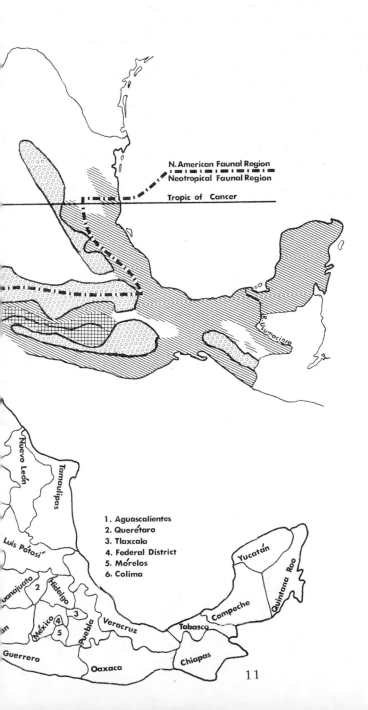

N. American Faunal Region
Neotropical Faunal Region

Tropic of Cancer

R. Usumacinta

Nuevo León

Tamaulipas

Luis Potosí

Guanajuato

Hidalgo

México

Morelos

Puebla

Veracruz

Tabasco

Guerrero

Oaxaca

Chiapas

Campeche

Yucatán

Quintana Roo

1. Aguascalientes
2. Querétaro
3. Tlaxcala
4. Federal District
5. Morelos
6. Colima

   In terms of zoogeography the nearctic and neotropical regions of America are divided along the U-shaped line just described, but in this book the southern political boundary of Mexico was chosen as our limit instead, since travelers are likely to visit the southernmost area, and the tropical species constitute an essential element in the family. Nor is the southernmost region entirely tropical, for there are large areas at higher altitude which comprise temperate pine-oak woodlands. There is again an East/West division, with the tropical deciduous forests being western and the tropical evergreen forests eastern (as is most of the true rain forest except for a narrow belt in the Sierra Madre de Chiapas). Some species and subspecies are confined to the western side, and some to the eastern, as would be expected. Map 2 illustrates the political subdivisions of Mexico. Map 3 illustrates the major cordilleras and the temperate and tropical regions of Mexico.

METRIC 20 40 60 80 100

Millimeters

1 2 3 4

Inches

2

THE SWALLOWTAIL FAMILY

Family Papilionidae

The first thing that one needs to know in order to use a family handbook is how to tell a member of the Swallowtail Family from other kinds of butterflies. Despite the name, the presence of tails is not a certain indication. The Dagger Wings, which may be seen in Florida, Texas and Mexico, have equally long tails but belong to the family Nymphalidae. On the other hand there is one *tailless* species of Swallowtail in the U.S.; and fifteen True Swallowtails in Mexico are without tails. The Pipevine Swallowtail exists in two forms, one tailed, and a rarer form without tails, while several species have tailed males and tailless females. So, despite the fact that most species have prominent tails, these cannot be a dependable sign of belonging to the family.

There is, however, a distinguishing mark for the family which is nearly as easy to see as a tail. The Papilionidae have only one anal (or vannal) vein, complete to margin, on each hind wing. (Some Aristolochia Swt. exhibit an additional, rudimentary anal vein.) To observe this point you will need to have a specimen in hand but, if you don't wish to collect it, any high school biology class is likely to have a few butterfly specimens. It is easier to see veins if one looks at the under side, and in the center of the hind wing will be seen a nearly continuous oval shaped vein, within which is the discal cell. Between this cell and the abdominal edge of the *hind* wing, if the butterfly is a Swallowtail

13

Family member, there will be only one vein stemming from the wing base and continuing to the outer margin (Fig. 2-1a). If there are two such veins the butterfly belongs to some other family. As for most rules there is one exception: the last species in this book (*Baronia brevicornis*) which belongs to the most distant past of the family, before the second vein was lost. Otherwise this lack is a perfect sign for family identification.

There is a second characteristic which applies to all members of the Swallowtail Family, but it is not readily visible and requires a 15X hand lens to see well. On the front legs of Papilionidae the second long joint (*tibia*) has a spur (*epiphysis*) that projects much like a rooster's, but it is proportionally quite small and droops downward (Fig. 2-2). This mark is more a technical point than a handy means of recognizing the family members, and the exception this time is that the Skippers also have such a spur; but that family is easily recognized by the head, which is much wider than high.

Figure 2-1. Anal veins. *a.* Single vein (Swallowtails). *b.* Two veins (all other butterflies).

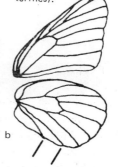

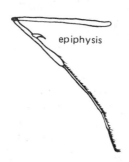

Figure 2-2. Spur (*epiphysis*) on foreleg of all Swallowtails.

Members of the family Pieridae, the Sulphurs and Whites, are close relatives of the Swallowtails, but the two anal veins in the hind wing readily separate them (Fig. 2-1b). The family Nymphalidae contains the butterflies most likely to be confused, as many of them are of large size, but they have an easy distinguishing mark: the front pair of legs is very much shrunken—less than half the size of the other two pairs—so that they are of no use for walking. Around the world there are a number of Swallowtails which mimic various species of the Nymphalidae and some are nearly perfect replicas, but the size of their forelegs distinguishes them at once. By some students the family Nymphalidae is divided into several families, making the Monarch group into the family Danaidae, and so on, but however divided all of these have the small forelegs.

The Coppers and Blues, family Lycanidae, are of small size and not likely to be confused, but in any case are distinguished by having antennae which arise from notches in the upper, inside corners of the eyes. Most of them have two anal veins on the hind wing, but a few Metalmarks have only one, providing another exception to that rule. The Snout Butterflies are a separate family but have only twelve species and are no problem; they can be distinguished by a beak-like development of the palps, which gives them their name.

The Swallowtails have yet another distinction and it is a highly visible one; but it pertains to the larvae of the family rather than to adult butterflies. The caterpillars of this family, uniquely, have a Y-shaped gland just behind the head which can be everted or retracted at will (Fig. 2-3). This organ, called an *osmeterium*, emits an odorous liquid which has a defensive purpose—although the smell is not always unpleasant from the human standpoint. It is very simple to get a caterpillar to evert these 'antlers' by pushing its body gently with the finger; and by the time of the caterpillar's second stage the osmeterium is quite visible. Color of the organ varies with the species, from white to yellow-brown, or orangish.

In our area caterpillars of all True Swallowtails (Papilioninae) possess this osmeterium—there is a Jamaican species in which it is lacking—and at least some members of the genus *Parnassius* (Parnassiinae) have osmeteria. For a long while there was great curiosity as to whether or not the very primitive *Baronia brevicornis* would possess the organ and when its early stages were first described (Vazquez & Perez 1961) the organ and the spot on the prothorax where it is sheathed were verified. This organ is not only unique but also gives one a perfect way to decide whether or not any caterpillar found in the wild belongs to the Swallowtail Family.

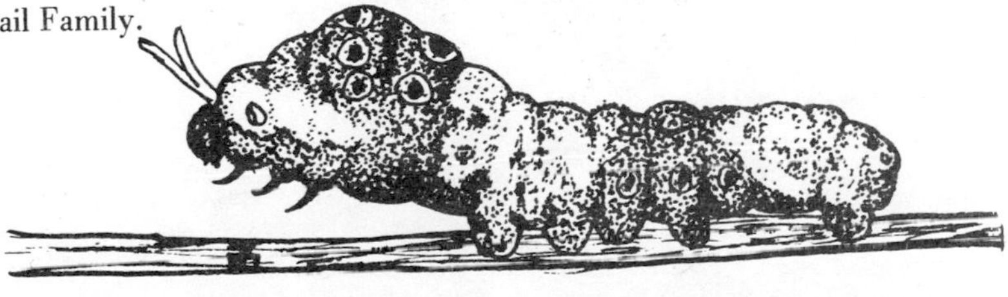

Figure 2-3. Caterpillar of Giant Swallowtail (*Papilio cresphontes*), showing osmeterium.

Most of the butterflies discussed in this book are True Swallowtails belonging to the subfamily Papilioninae. All members of this subfamily have a distinguishing mark which is apparently not found in any other family of butterflies and it is lacking or rudimentary in the other two subfamilies of Papilionidae. The mark consists of a very short crossvein at the base of the forewing, connecting the anal vein and the discal cell (Figs. 2-1a and 2-4). Although this vein may be less than one eighth of an inch it is very readily seen if the forewing is viewed from the under surface. With the addition of this mark to what has gone before, the three sub-families of Swallowtails may be distinguished as follows:

I. **True Swallowtails** (Papilioninae) (1) to (63)
Crossvein at base of forewing present; only one anal vein on hind wing.

II. **The Parnassians** (Parnassiinae) (64) to (66)
No crossvein on forewing; only one anal vein on hindwing.

III. **The Baron** (Baroniinae) (67)
No crossvein on forewing; two anal veins on hindwing.

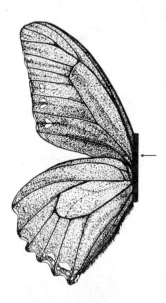

Figure 2-4. Crossvein in forewing of True Swallowtails.

Having first noted how to tell members of the family Papilionidae from other butterflies and then how to discriminate the subfamilies within the Swallowtails, we would find it convenient if there were equally simple ways to discriminate the four different genera of True Swallowtails in our selected area. Unfortunately the simplest table of these differences requires close attention, a hand lens, and some practice. While the table below will not be particularly useful to beginners, some of them may grow into its use as they study the Swallowtails. The best approach is to select known specimens from each genus, and for three of the four that is easily done. For the genus *Papilio* take a Tiger Swallowtail; for the genus *Eurytides* a Zebra Swallowtail; a Pipevine Swallowtail will do for the genus *Battus*. The fourth genus, *Parides*, has only a record or two for *P. arcas* in Texas, but there are several common species in Mexico. By matching specimens with the features noted in the table one will soon begin to grasp the comparative points.

Key for Discriminating the Four Genera

A. Rows of spines on underside of *tarsi* separated from rows on top by a sharply defined, spineless, impressed space.
   1. Abdominal margin of hind wing rolled downward, giving the appearance of being fluted when viewed from beneath; no scent fold on inner edge of hind wing in males.
      = genus *Papilio*—Fluted Swallowtails
   2. Abdominal margin of hind wing not rolled down. On males this margin is elaborated, usually bearing a scent organ within a pocket folded upward and over the wing, or at least a vestige of this fold is present.
      = genus *Eurytides*—Kites

B. Rows of spines on *tarsi* not separated by a spineless, impressed space.
   1. Antennae with sharply defined sensory grooves. Scent fold on abdominal margin of hind wing of males contains woolly matter inside. No naked streak between fold and discal cell.
      = genus *Parides*—the Cattle Hearts
   2. Antennae without distinct sensory grooves. Scent fold never contains woolly matter. A naked streak between fold and discal cell.
      = genus *Battus*—the Gold Rims

WHEN TO COLLECT AND WHEN NOT TO COLLECT

Even if one doesn't expect to carry a study of Swallowtails as far as the above chart anticipates, it will be helpful to collect at least a few butterflies to learn the points by which they are distinguished, and that brings one to the questions of endangered species, and conservation. Around the world butterflies are greatly endangered both by aerial spraying with pesticides and by the destruction of their natural habitats. There are probably some kinds that are endangered by collecting for ornamental display objects and jewelry—the blue Morphos particularly are under this pressure—but there are few that are endangered by collecting for study, even very amateur study. Of the Swallowtails considered in this book only Schaus's Swallowtail, from islands off Florida, has a tenuous hold, and certainly females of that race should be let alone. There are other rare species or races, but their very rareness protects them and they are seldom found in collections because their lives are lived briefly in places difficult to reach.

A few facts will put the matter into perspective. A female Swallowtail may lay from 150 to 250 eggs, [and Steven Sims (personal communication) has found that some *Papilio zelicaon* females lay over 350 eggs.] To maintain a population balance it is necessary that only one male and one female from that number survive and mate to produce another generation. If very many survive from each batch of eggs there will be a population explosion, since the 100 females that could potentially survive in the second brood would become 10,000 females in the next. Since males are not needed for breeding on a one-to-one basis in any case, and as most females seen are likely to have already laid eggs, the collecting of a few adult specimens has little effect on over-all population numbers.

The same is not at all true when it comes to collecting early stages. Swallowtails tend to breed in localized pockets even when their general distribution is broad. They will prefer some particular road or stream and lay eggs here and there along that route, which becomes home for one colony, generation after generation. When these specific places are found, and the food plant is known, it is easy to gather up the larvae in numbers and if that is done by several collectors, year after year, it may reduce the colony's numbers below the safety margin. This seems to have happened to the *Papilio indra pergamus* colony in the canyon behind the city of Santa Barbara in California. The *species* is not at all in danger, nor is this subspecies, but that particular colony seems to have been wiped out by overcollection of eggs and larvae. One certainly doesn't want that to happen often.

There are ways in which a butterfly collector can more than make up for the individuals he has extracted. Many butterflies are readily encouraged to live in gardens by providing for their needs. These consist of the flowers adults use for food: lilac, philadelphus, butterfly bush, abelia, zinnias, stocks, wallflowers, mints, clovers, tithonia, and Michaelmas daisies, which are all sought for their nectars. Pools of water or puddles on the ground are also needed, and of course the specific larval food plants for each kind. With all of these inducements it is possible to maintain tenfold the normal population of butterflies in a garden, and the gardener's reward is thus a tenfold increase in beauty. For the species which do not like civilization and garden comforts it is still possible to raise the caterpillars at home and then return the pupae to their natural habitat before the time of emergence the following year. Hand raised and sheltered groups have a much higher survival rate through the winter, so the colony will be strengthened by your efforts, to say nothing of what you will have learned in the process.

HILLTOPPING AND PATROLLING

Hilltopping seems to be a habit characteristic of Swallowtails although by no means limited to them. Ants of some species, flies, and dragonflies, have members which are hilltoppers, as have several families of butterflies. Skippers often congregate on mountain tops, as do certain Nymphalids such as the Red Admiral and the Painted Lady. To observe this phenomenon all that is necessary is to look around the local horizon for some particular hill which stands out above others, then take yourself to the top of it some April morning. As the day warms up you will begin to see a host of butterflies streaming to the hill top. The males of some species will be observed choosing and defending territories in which they investigate other species which pass, and fight their own kind if they intrude.

One of the demonstrated purposes of such hilltop gatherings is mating. Shields (1967) was able to prove, by catching all butterflies which appeared on a hill, that most of the hilltoppers were males and that all females there were unfertilized. Presumably these depart as soon

19

as mated and the arrangement makes it simple for any female to locate a mate. The newly emerged female has only to strike out for the most prominent hill in her field of vision. It is interesting that hilltopping species which have spread into flat country will continue to use any rise in the terrain, particularly if it is capped by a clump of trees, as though it were a real mountain, or they will even use man-made objects such as a radio transmitting tower. A friend traveling in Germany noted only a few Old-World Swallowtails in a village, but when he climbed up to the local castle he found a great number of these butterflies patrolling the castle walls!

While a number of species in the genera *Papilio* and *Eurytides* are hilltoppers it is within the Old-World Swallowtail group that this becomes a prime habit. In fact so much is this true that some of the mountains have to be divided up. Where the Anise and Indra Swallowtails fly together the Anise will always occupy the very peak, while Indra patrols the rim areas on the southern and western slopes of the mountain. "Hilltopping" in these instances often involves mountains of 9000 feet or more. Since the larval food plants of these two species are found on the slopes of the same mountains, and not uncommonly on ridges and peaks, it has been suggested that the search for larval food plants is a motive in hilltopping. That motive would scarcely apply to the males in any case; and the Pale Swallowtail, which is the most notable hilltopper in the Tiger Swallowtail group, will hilltop in the Sierra Nevada of California at altitudes far above those of its food plant.

It is worthy of note that the Western Tiger Swallowtail (which often flies with the Pale Swallowtail) and the Two-tailed Tiger Swallowtail use a different approach to meeting and mating. The males of these species patrol up and down a section of stream or river, keeping right on the water course. Then all the newly hatched female has to do is locate the nearest water course and flutter along its edges until patrolling males notice her. Prof. A. M. Shapiro notes (private communication) that on the tree-lined city streets of Davis, Calif., *Papilio rutulus* behaves in exactly the same way, suggesting that "the linear habitat defined by trees is the critical factor, *not* the water."

That this observation is probably correct is indicated by another version of patrolling practiced by the tropical Cattle Hearts of the genus *Parides.* Species of this genus inhabit dense tropical forests, and there the males choose a segment of trail through the jungle and patrol it back

20

and forth on a beat limited by other males at either end. Sunlight rather than water attracts the female Cattle Heart to trails, and once mated she returns to the jungle in search of Aristolochia vines on which to lay her eggs. The Kite Swallowtails of the genus *Eurytides* are vigorous hilltoppers, and those among them known as White-Pages make long-distance flights, high in the air and at speed, over forests toward outstanding mountains.

An instructive task for any beginning entomologist is to select some hill and keep track of which species congregate, and when. The composition of the assemblage will shift with both time of day and the passage of days. Swallowtails are seemingly most active from ten in the morning until midday, while the Nymphalids are afternoon hilltoppers. It will be noted that in the evening all of the Swallowtails descend at least to the lower slopes of the hills, where they roost for the night. The males of some species are quite violent when establishing their territories and one can hear the clicking noise made by the clash of forewings when male Anise Swallowtails joust. The losers in this species give up quickly, but it is said that Indra males of the Colorado subspecies will fight until both contestants are in tatters.

SCIENTIFIC NAMES

The more serious student will wish to learn the scientific names of at least some of this family of butterflies, and these are for the most part derived from Greek which has been Latinized. It is very difficult to learn something meaningless, so the system behind Swallowtail names is worth noting. Linnaeus, who originated the modern system of naming plants and animals, had a particular unity in mind for the nomenclature of this group of butterflies. He placed all Swallowtails, and a number of quite different kinds, in the genus *Papilio*, which was simply the Latin name for butterflies in general, and decided to name each species after one of the heroes of the Trojan war. He took his names from Homer, beginning by calling the type species *machaon*, after the surgeon of the Greek forces. *Papilio machaon* is the common Old-World Swallowtail of Europe. As other species were named this procedure was generally followed, except that later scientists, running short of heroes, reached farther into Greek and Roman mythology. When the French naturalist, Latreille, erected the genus *Parnassius* he, in turn, named the type species *apollo*. We don't have that species here, but we do have

Parnassius phoebus and Phoebus is another name for Apollo, so now we have both these creatures flitting around the peak of the sacred mountain and its god.

The names of most North American species are in this tradition, and sometimes related species make sense as a name group. According to Virgil, Turnus, son of Daunus, was king of a Roman tribe called Rutulus. These are the names of the Eastern Tiger, the Two-tailed and the Western Tiger Swallowtail. Or they were, but for reasons of priority the first (*turnus*) was changed to *glaucus*—which is not bad, as that son of King Minos wore golden armor while fighting at Troy—but the name *daunus* was changed to *multicaudatus*; *rutulus* endures in current use. The Pale Swallowtail of the same group was named for Eurymedon, king of the giants; and Pilumnus was a Roman god of corn-grinding. Troilus was a son of Priam, King of Troy, while Palamedes fought on the Greek side and is credited with the invention of lighthouses.

To anticipate Chapter 3, Polyxenes, like Machaon, was with the Greek army, but Indra and Nitra are both names of the chief of the Vedic (Hindu) gods, "the shining one". The names in Chapter 6 are: Cresphontes, a descendant of Heracles, Thoas a companion of Odysseus, Androgeus a brother of Glaucus, Astyalas a Trojan knight, Ornythion a Corinthian king, Aristodemus a king of Sparta, and Andraemon the father of Thoas. In Chapter 8, Anchisiades is another name for Aeneas, while Idaeus was King Priam's charioteer; Torquatus was a Roman consul, but the name is probably a tribute to the Italian poet, Torquato Tasso. Garamas was one of the first children of Mother Earth, Abderus a son of Hermes, and Electryon a son of Perseus.

In Chapter 9 we come to the new genus, *Eurytides*, which was named for one of the heroes of the Calydonian boar-hunt. Within this genus we find Marcellus who opposed Hannibal, Philolaus the brother of Eurymedon, and Branchus who fathered a wicked wrestler killed by Theseus. Thymbraeus was a son of Laocoon, and his death was a portent to the Trojans, while Protesilaus was a knight killed by Aeneas; Calliste was both a nymph of and another name for Artemis. Three names in the genus are outside the mythic tradition: the Lacandones are an Indian tribe of Chiapas, Salvin was the great naturalist who studied Central America, and Marchand was simply a gentleman of Chartres.

Parides possibly means 'of Paros', while Battus was a rustic whom Hermes turned into a touchstone. Specifically, Polydamas was a Trojan leader, Belus a king of Egypt, Iphidamas a son of Antenor, and Arcas a son of Zeus by Calliste. So if one is trying to memorize some of these difficult scientific names he should be encouraged by knowing that they are not meaningless and that each one does have a story behind it, even though it will not tell one much about the butterfly.

A few words may help those unfamiliar with the forms of scientific names. The capitalized name in italics is the name of the genus, while the second italicized name, which has no capital, is that of the species. These are followed by a man's name and a date, indicating who first described the species and when. If this name is in parenthesis it indicates that he described the species, but did not place it in the present genus. For example, *Battus polydamas* (L.) 1758: Linnaeus (L) described *polydamas* but placed it in *Papilio*. As that genus has subsequently been subdivided, *polydamas* is now assigned to the genus *Battus*. Knowing the author of the species and the date he described it allows one to find his original description.

When there is a third italicized name, following the genus and species, it indicates a subspecies, or geographical race as it is sometimes called. Any other variation has no real standing and is called a form, and if it has a name this is placed in quotes and not italicized. For example the very dark form of the Black Swallowtail would be listed as *Papilio polyxenes* f. "ampliata". Seasonal variations are handled in the same way, such as adding "ver. f." for vernal (spring) form, etc. Several of the Old-World Swallowtail group have both yellow and dark forms of the same species, but these are not subspecies even though they have sometimes been listed as such.

PLATE I

1. Alaskan Old World Swallowtail, *Papilio machaon aliaska* ♂ (1). Haines Junction, Yukon Terr. 15 June 1967.

2. Under surface of same specimen.

3. Hudsonian Old World Swallowtail, *Papilio machaon hudsonianus* ♂ (1). No data. Under surface. Note bulbous expansion at end of margin in anal eye spot.

4. Black Swallowtail, *Papilio polyxenes asterius* ♀ (2). Harrisburg, Penn. 20 July 1974.

5. *Papilio polyxenes asterius* ♂ (2) Presidio, Mexico. June 1943. Spots of median band slightly reduced in size.

6. *Papilio polyxenes asterius* ♂, f. "ampliata" (2). State of Guerrero, Mexico. September 1969. No yellow median band on UpFW.

7. *Papilio polyxenes asterius* ♂, f. "pseudoamericus" (2). Catemaco, Veracruz, Mexico. 16 April 1972. This specimen is an extreme of yellow form; UpHW often has black base.

PLATE II

1. Baird's Swallowtail, *Papilio bairdii* ♂ (5). Barton Flats, San Bernardino Co., Calif. 30 July 1966.

2. *Papilio bairdii* ♀ (5). Barton Flats, San Bernardino Co., Calif. 29 July 1966.

3.a. Bruce's Swallowtail, *Papilio bairdii* f. "brucei" ♂ (5). 1 mi. S of Texas Creek, Fremont Co., Colo. 17 July 1970. Pupil of "eye-spot" of this ♂ atypical; ♀♀ taken with it had usual connecting bar from margin to pupil as in Fig. 1.
  b. Under surface of same specimen. Note reduced yellow on outer areas of both wings, compared to *P. oregonius*, Fig. 5.

4. Anise Swallowtail, *Papilio zelicaon* ♂ (8). Los Angeles, Calif. 2 August 1961.

5.a. Oregon Swallowtail, *Papilio oregonius* ♂ (6). Brewster, Washington. 7 July 1955.
  b. Under surface of same specimen.

6. Rudkin's Swallowtail, *Papilio rudkini* ♂ (10). Providence Mts., San Bernardino Co., Calif. 3 June 1968.

PLATE I

1

2

3

4

5

6

7

PLATE II

PLATE III

1. Short-tailed Swallowtail, *Papilio brevicauda* ♀ (4). Newfoundland. Summer 1965.

2. Nitra Swallowtail, *Papilio nitra* ♂ (9). Montana, 1961. (Not the ♂ described in text.)

3. Indra Swallowtail, *Papilio indra indra* ♂ (11). Green Mountain, Boulder Co., Colo. 27 May 1974.

4 Ford's Swallowtail, *Papilio indra fordi* ♂ (11). Granite Mts., Mojave Desert, San Bernardino Co., Calif. May 1970.

5. Nevada Swallowtail, *Papilio indra nevadensis* ♀ (11). Jett Canyon, Toiyabe Range, Nye Co., Nevada. 26 May 1974. Coll.: Marc Grinnell.

6. Edwards' Swallowtail, *Papilio indra pergamus* ♂ (11). Laguna Mts., San Diego Co., Calif. April 1961.

PLATE IV

1. Eastern Tiger Swallowtail, *Papilio glaucus* ♂ (12). Harrisburg, Penn. 20 July 1974.

2. Canadian Tiger Swallowtail, *Papilio glaucus canadensis* ♂ (12). Fairbanks, Alaska. 9 June 1962.

3. Western Tiger Swallowtail, *Papilio rutulus* ♂ (13). Malibu Canyon, Los Angeles Co., Calif. June 1961.

4. Under surface of same specimen. Note that yellow submarginal spots of UnFW form continuous band; UnHW uppermost submarginal spot is yellow.

5. *Papilio glaucus,* under surface. Note that spots of UnFW submarginal band are separate; UnHW uppermost submarginal spot orange. (12)

6. Two-tailed Swallowtail, *Papilio multicaudatus* ♂ (16). Ciudad Victoria, Tamaulipas, Mexico. 20 May 1971.

7. *Papilio glaucus* ♀, yellow form (12). Same data as Fig. 1.

8. *Papilio glaucus* ♀, dark form (12). Harrisburg, Penn. July 1974.

PLATE III

1

2

3

4

5

30

6

PLATE IV

1

2

3

4

5

6

7

8

PLATE V

1. Pale Swallowtail, *Papilio eurymedon* ♂ (15). Near Griffith Observatory, Los Angeles Co., Calif. May 1966.

2. Three-tailed Swallowtail, *Papilio pilumnus* ♂ (17). Ochuc, Chiapas, Mexico. 12 July 1972.

3. Spicebush Swallowtail, *Papilio troilus* ♂ (18). Linglestown, Dauphin Co., Penn. June 1973.

4. *Papilio troilus* ♀ (18). Loysville, Penn. July 1956.

5. Palamedes Swallowtail, *Papilio palamedes* ♀ (19). Miami, Florida. May 1954.

6.a. Mexican Tiger Swallowtail, *Papilio alexiares* ♂ (14). Drawn from plate in Godman and Salvin, *Biologia Centrali-Americana: Insecta: Lepidoptera—Rhopalocera*.

  b. Under surface; the orange streaks are diagnostic.

PLATE VI

1. Giant Swallowtail, *Papilio cresphontes pennsylvanicus* ♀ (20). Pinclo Park, York Co., Penn. July 1968.

2. Thoas Swallowtail, *Papilio thoas* ♂ (21). Quintana Roo, Yucatan Pen., Mexico. 24 August 1964. Mexican specimens usually lack yellow spot in UpFW cell—see text.

3. Schaus's Swallowtail, *Papilio aristodemus ponceanus* ♀ (25). Small Florida Key. May 1959.

4. Diaz Swallowtail, *Papilio diazi* ♂ (34). Tepoztlan, Morelos, Mexico. Drawn from color photograph of one of the original specimens, supplied by Alberto Diaz Frances.

5. Pallas Swallowtail, *Papilio astyalus pallas* ♂ (23). Cotaxtla Riv., Veracruz, Mexico. September 1973.

6. *Papilio astyalus pallas* ♀ (23). Quintana Roo, Yucatan Pen., Mexico. August 1964.

PLATE V

1

2

3

4

5

6

34

a

b

PLATE VI

35

PLATE VII

1. Androgeus Swallowtail, *Papilio androgeus epidaurus* ♂ (24). Oaxaca, Mexico. 20 July 1970.

2. *Papilio androgeus epidaurus* ♀ (24). (Yucatan, Mexico. June 1962) ? The extensi light patch of FW is characteristic of a ♀ form from zil; patch is usually lacking in Mexican specimens.

3. Bahaman Swallowtail, *Papilio andraemon bonhotei* ♂ (26). Bahamas (island unknown). April 1967.

4. *Papilio androgeus epidaurus* ♀ (24). Oaxaca, Mexico. May 1971. The common ♀ form in Mexico.

5. King Ornython Swallowtail, *Papilio ornython* ♀ (22). Ciudad Mante, Tamaulipas, Mexico. May 1971.

6. *Papilio ornython* ♂ (?2). Ciudad Victoria, Tamaulipas, Mexico, 28 May 1969.

PLATE VIII

1. Idaeus Swallowtail, *Papilio anchisiades idaeus* ♂ (27). Yucatan, Mexico. January 1961.

2. *Papilio anchisiades idaeus* ♂. Variant form (27). San Quintin, Chiapas. 3 September 1970.

3. Roger's Swallowtail, *Papilio rogeri* ♂ (31). Pisté, Yucatan, Mexico. 24 July 1967.

4. Pharnaces Swallowtail, *Papilio pharnaces* ♂ (28). Mexicali River, Guerrero, Mexico. August 1942. a. upper surface; b. under surface.

5. Cupid's Quilt Swallowtail, *Papilio erostratus* ♂ (29). Comitán, Chiapas, Mexico. July 1956.

6. *Papilio erostratus* ♀ (29). Acozinco, Chiapas, Mexico. August 1968.

7. Vazquez Swallowtail, *Papilio erostratinus* ♂ (30). Jalapa, Veracruz, Mexico, at 1500 m (5000 ft). August 1974.

8. *Papilio erostratinus* ♀ (30). Jalapa, Veracruz, Mexico.

PLATE VII

PLATE VIII

1

2

3

a   4   b

5

6

7

8

I

THE TRUE SWALLOWTAILS

Subfamily PAPILIONINAE

The True Swallowtails are much the largest subfamily in the Papilionidae, with nearly five hundred species, distributed over five continents. Considered together, the species which make up the subfamily **Papilioninae** are adaptable, and have been most successful in adjusting to a wide variety of habitats in both temperate and tropical regions. In the area covered by this book the **Papilioninae** comprise four genera, of which the Fluted Swallowtails, belonging to the genus *Papilio*, are of worldwide distribution. The Kite Swallowtails are also found worldwide, though scientists divide them between two genera: *Eurytides*, for the American Kites, and *Graphium*, for the Old World species. The Cattle Hearts make up a third genus, *Parides*, which has members in the New World, and also in the Oriental and Indo-Australian regions. The fourth genus, *Battus*, the Gold Rims, is found only in the New World.

THE FLUTED SWALLOWTAILS

Genus **Papilio** L. 1758

The North American Fluted Swallowtails of the genus *Papilio* were divided by Rothschild and Jordan (1906) into seven groups, and scientists have since kept this arrangement. Each group comprises closely related species which differ from those in other groups, but do not differ distinctly enough for each group to be treated as a subgenus. In this book, without changing their order, these seven groups are brought into four chapters.

3

THE OLD WORLD SWALLOWTAIL AND ITS NEW WORLD RELATIVES

The Old World Swallowtail group has the distinction of being the only Swallowtail group in the New World with relatives in Europe and Asia close enough to have had immediate common ancestors. The Alaskan Swallowtail, which also ranges across Canada, is the same species, *Papilio machaon*, as the Swallowtail found all across Asia, and across all Europe, from Lapland in the north to the Mediterranean and North Africa in the south, as far west as England. Linking of the two hemispheres in this circumboreal manner is unique to this species in the family, and adaptation to northern, boreal conditions is also unusual among Swallowtails. The vast majority of species in the family Papilionidae are tropical, so it is assumed to be of tropical origin, with the implication that the few kinds adapted to extremely cold regions reached those areas secondarily.

In the Old World this group comprises only two other species, both of them in southern temperate regions: *P. hospiton* from the islands of Corsica and Sardinia, and *P. alexanor* from the south of France, southern Italy, the Balkans, and as far east as Turkestan. In Japan there is a subspecies which may deserve the rank of species; but all told the number of species is small for the vastness and diversity of the Old World range of the group. In North America, on the other hand, the group has differentiated into a number of species and potential species. As some of them are still in the process of speciation, the number of full species is still an open question. All that have been listed as species by some competent modern authority are presented (with one exception) in this chapter as species, although it seems likely that of these eleven, four or five may prove to be subspecies, or merely forms. In any case, information on distribution, food plants and the like is valid whatever eventual decision may be made on their status.

As a group these American species are adapted to the colder regions of Alaska and Canada, or to the mountains of the western U.S. where conditions are similar. However, the individual species may show broad tolerance. The Anise Swallowtail is equally able to thrive in the high mountains, or along the warm coast of southern California, and the Indra Swallowtail has subspecies specialized for various habitats, from high mountains to low deserts. The Black Swallowtail, familiar in the eastern U.S., has also made its way down the plateaus and mountains of Mexico and Central America to the western part of South America, to become the only widespread American member of this group.

Since the black-and-yellow color combination of this group is repeated in the Tiger Swallowtails, the visual distinctions should be kept in mind:

Old World Swt. Group: The black lines on yellow ground follow along veins from black base to black borders. No black V on HW. (The European *P. alexanor* is an exception.)

Tiger Swt. Group: The black lines or bars crossing yellow ground color are basically vertical and cut across veins. HW with vertical black V.

All species of the Old World Swallowtail group in America have the same basic pattern, which makes them comparatively difficult to identify, but the pattern sorts out into two opposites, producing either yellow butterflies with black markings, or black butterflies with yellow markings. The black effect is achieved by reducing the width of the yellow median band until it becomes merely a row of yellow spots, such as one sees on the Black Swallowtail. How little difference in the basic pattern there really is can be seen in a form of the Black Swallowtail found mostly in Mexico. In f. "pseudoamericus" (see Pl. I, Fig. 7) the yellow band of the HW is not reduced and the result is a specimen that at a distance would easily pass for an Anise Swallowtail.

OLD WORLD SWALLOWTAIL GROUP

1.   *Papilio machaon aliaska* Scudder 1869

ALASKAN OLD WORLD SWALLOWTAIL   Pl. 1, Figs. 1, 2.

Expanse: 65-70 mm   **Tails:** 4-5 mm

Description. Sexes similar. UpFW: Yellow median band; black base heavily dusted with gold scales; discal cell black with two yellow bars; broad black wing margin with submarginal row of yellow spots. UpHW: Yellow median band extends through cell; inner margin black to cell; broad black outer margin with yellow fringe spots and submarg. row of yellow lunules, inside which is a row of blue spots. Anal "eye" spot red, without black "pupil". UnFW: Yellow submarg. spots united to form a yellow band. Distinctions: from other species of group, by lack of pupil in eye spot; separated from subspecies *hudsonianus* by wider outer black border of HW which comes closer to cell, and no tendency of the margin of eye spot to end as a bulb.

Habitat: In or near forests in mountainous areas, but also in sparsely wooded country, and on tundra at sea level.

Flight. June and July.

Food Plants. (Throughout the book this heading refers to *larval* food sources.) Members of Parsley family (Umbelliferae); reputedly also Arctic sagebrush (*Artemisia arctica*).

Early Stages. Mature larva has yellow head with oval black spot on face, and black streaks down either side; body yellow-green to green, with black lines between segments and wide black bands with red or orange dots on them on each segment; osmeterium red-orange.

Distribution and Subspecies.

1.a.   *P. machaon aliaska* (*P. machaon machaon* is n. European)

As described above.

Distribution. Seward Pen.; Ramparts on Yukon R.; Koyukuk R. (67-69 N x 151 W); Point Barrow; Noluck Lake; Sagwon; Haines; Kavik R. Yukon Terr.: Kluane Lake; Mayo; Haines Junction. N.W. Terr.: Tununuk Pt.; Inuvik. B.C.: Atlin, in nw. corner of prov.

1.b.   *P. machaon hudsonianus* Clark 1932

HUDSONIAN OLD WORLD SWALLOWTAIL   Pl. I, Fig. 3.

Description. Basically as above but averages larger. Distinguished by
having long yellow hairs on abdomen, and margin of eye spot
enlarged or bulbous at end. Often the UnFW submarg. spots are
separated rather than in a band. On these points see Clark (1932)
and McDunnough (1934).
Habitat. Coniferous forest.
Flight. From late May to July.
Distribution. Starting in se. Canada: Cochrane, n. Ontario, N to James
Bay (Rupert House); up w. side of Hudson Bay to Nelson R. in
Manitoba.   S from Cochrane to Thunder Bay area of Lake
Superior; 5 mi. SW of Ft. Williams being the southern-most record.
Manitoba: Berens R. along L. Winnipeg; Riding Mts. in W of
province; and Lynn Lake in far N. Saskatchewan: Locally com-
mon in N, S to Duck Mtn. Park, Porcupine Plain, and Paddock-
wood.   Northern Alberta.   Northwest Terr.   There is a record
from Ft. McPherson on the Peel R.   If valid, the range of this
subsp. overlaps on the north the range of *P. m. aliaska* in Yukon
Terr.

1.c.   *P. machaon dodi* McDunnough 1939

CYPRESS HILLS OLD WORLD SWALLOWTAIL

Description. Slightly larger than *hudsonianus* and without yellow hairs
on abdomen.   ♂ has wide yellow band on either side of abdomen
with a black line near base.   ♀ has more orange on under side of
wings; bulb at end of eye spot border is large and takes up more
of eye.
Habitat. Hills where n. slopes are coniferous.
Distribution. Cypress Hills of s. Saskatch. to the Rocky Mts. in Alberta.
Note. Some students have suggested that *P. m. hudsonianus* and *P. m.
dodi* might be closer to the Anise Swt. than to the Alaskan Swt.

2.   *Papilio polyxenes* Fabricius 1775

BLACK SWALLOWTAIL   Pl. I, Figs. 4, 5.

Expanse: 65-90 mm   **Tails:** 7-10 mm

Description. Sexes differ somewhat. UpFW: Black with median row of triangular, base-out, apex-in, yellow spots; cell black with at least a trace of yellow bar at apex; yellow fringe and submarg. spots. UpHW: Median band of irregular yellow spots which cross outer end of cell in ♂ and bypass it in ♀; between band and submarg. yellow spots there is a row of blue spots which are larger in ♀; anal eye spot orange and centered with a round black pupil; margin of eye spot incomplete at rear. UnFW: Median spots generally washed with orange, as are those of HW except two lunules between tail and eye spot. Abdomen black, with rows, generally two, of yellow dots on each side.

Habitat: Meadows, open fields, cultivated lands, barnyards, parks. Likes cities; doesn't like forests, but will fly in either dry uplands or low marshes. Adults are everywhere partial to clover, alfalfa and thistle blooms. In Mexico inhabits pine-oak woodland.

Flight. February to Oct. or Nov. in far S where there are three broods. Early May to Sept. in Wisconsin, with two broods. Three broods in Delaware Valley, Penn.: April-May, June-July, Aug.-Sept.

Food Plants. Members of Parsley family (Umbelliferae): garden dill, carrot, fennel—in Mexico on naturalized fennel—wild carrot; in Colo. *Harbouria trachypleura. Thamnosma texana*, Rue family.

Early Stages. Mature larva bright green, with black bands containing yellow spots on each segment.

Distribution and Subspecies.

2.a.   *P. polyxenes asterius* Stoll 1782 (*P. p. polyxenes* is Cuban)

At present this is the only subspecies in our area, but Colo. collectors feel that the population of the eastern foothills, up to about 7000 ft is a good subsp. as yet unnamed. The species: from s. Canada to Colombia, Ecuador and n. Peru. *P. p. asterius:* s. Canada as far west as se. Saskatchewan. All states east of Rockies in U.S. All of Mexico includ. Baja Calif. Western edge of U.S. distrib.: In Wyo. E of Continental Divide in Carbon, Albany and Converse Cos. (se. quarter of state). Colo.: all cos. E of continental divide and on w. side only N of the La Plata-San Juan Mt. ranges. In New Mexico it appears to skirt around s. end of Rockies. It is uncommon in the Sandia and Manzano Mts. to E of Albuquerque, but common on Ladron Peak S of there. In Ariz.

it flies in se. quarter of state, as far W as Tucson and as far N as the Mogollon Rim.

Forms. There are several named forms of which three are distinct and likely to be met. They are largely Mexican, but the first two may be found in s. Ariz., New Mexico, Texas, and occasionally elsewhere.

f. "ampliata" Ménétriés 1857

Very dark in both sexes, with median rows of spots obsolete and submarg. dots reduced. (See Pl. I, Fig. 6.)

f. "curvifascia" Skinner 1902

Median bands broad; HW without spot at end of cell in both sexes; wings and tails shorter. Type locality, Rincon, New Mexico.

f. "pseudoamericus" Brown 1942

Wide yellow bands equal to those of Anise Swt. The type is from Troy, Ill.; it occurs rarely anywhere, though more often in s. Ariz. and commonly in e. Mexico. (See Pl. I, Fig. 7.)

3. *Papilio kahli* Chermock & Chermock 1937

THE KAHLI SWALLOWTAIL

Expanse: 60-75 mm   **Tails:** 6-7 mm

Description. Sexes differ. Resembles the Black Swallowtail closely; pupil of anal eye spot displaced to rear edge of eye, sometimes connected to margin. The ♀ displays increased yellow markings, which is just the opposite of Black Swt. ♀.

Habitat. Bare hilltops.

Flight. May and June.

Food Plants. Cow parsnip (*Heracleum* spp.); and garden parsnips.

Early Stages. No description available.

Distribution. Central Manitoba N to The Pas, W to Punnichy, Sask., and S to Carnduff, Sask., Canada.

Note. Species status doubtful; some think the population is formed of hybrids between *P. machaon* (1) and *P. polyxenes* (2). Dos Passos (1964) placed a form called "avinoffi" under *P. machaon*; Hooper (1973) suggests that it may be a yellow form of *P. kahli*, and if the latter is a hybrid there could be a percentage of yellow forms.

4.   *Papilio brevicauda* Saunders 1869

SHORT-TAILED SWALLOWTAIL   Pl. III, Fig. 1.

Expanse: 70-85 mm   **Tails:** 2 mm

Description. Sexes similar. Resembles Black Swt. except that median band of upper side is wider and flushed with orange. (In Black Swt. only under side has orange wash.) The very short and broad tail is best distinction.

Habitat. Both dense coniferous forests and grassy seashore cliffs.

Flight. June and July; single-brooded.

Food Plants. Cow parsnip (*Heracleum* spp.); Scotch lovage (*Ligusticum scothicum*).

Early Stages. Mature larva pale green, with black bands on which there are yellow spots. The Breton subspecies pupates among or even under stones along the beach, the only instance of ground pupation by True Swallowtails of our area.

Distribution and Subspecies.

4.a.   *P. brevicauda brevicauda*

As described above. This is the largest race and has the most orange. Newfoundland and Anticosti Island.

4.b.   *P. b. bretonensis* McDunnough 1939

Smaller, and showing less orange. Baddeck, Cape Breton Is. New Brunswick, incl. Prince Edward Is. Mainland Nova Scotia.

4.c.   *P. b. gaspeensis* McDunnough 1934

The smallest race; median bands narrower, esp. on HW, and no orange on these spots on upper side. Slopes of Mt. Lyall, Gaspé Co., Quebec, about 40 miles inland at 1500 ft in heavy spruce forest.

Douglas Ferguson (1950) of the Nova Scotia Museum gave an account of his search for the Breton race. After years of failure he found the adults, eggs and larvae on Cape Breton Island in the first week of July. Breton Swallowtails fly together with the Black Swallowtail, but do not interbreed. The larval food plant grows in isolated clusters just above high tide mark along the sea-shore; the females fly along the cliffs and beaches to lay eggs on the scattered lovage. These butterflies have a peculiar habit of flying close to the ground, and when frightened their escape route is over the cliffs and down toward the ocean. Most Swallow-tails of the Old World group fly straight upward when alarmed.

It should be emphasized that the Short-tailed and its very close relative the Black Swallowtail fly together, and that when two species or forms occur together the situation is called *sympatric*. If they do not occur together, as with the Black and the Alaskan Swallowtails, the situation is called *allopatric*. On the western edge of its range the Black Swallowtail overlaps in some places with another near relative, Baird's Swallowtail, and at least in Colorado there is a peculiarity about the overlap. While both species occur in some of the same areas they have a different time sequence. For example, in Fremont Co. the Black Swallowtail is flying in June, while Baird's Swallowtail is still in the larval stages at that time. This staggering of breeding time spans, which tends to provide reproductive isolation, is called a *sympatric-allochronic* situation.

5.   *Papilio bairdii*   Edwards 1866

BAIRD'S SWALLOWTAIL   Pl. II, Figs. 1, 2.

Expanse: 75-90 mm   **Tails:** 8-11 mm
Description (of typical or black form). Sexes differ. The ♂ is much like eastern Black Swt., but can be separated by the pupil in the anal eye spot, which is displaced to the rear, club shaped, and often attached to the margin by a horizontal bar. (In Black Swt. the pupil is round and centered.) On underside of wings this species has pure yellow spots in median and submarg. rows of FW. When there are exceptions the fulvous is dull rather than bright orange as in Black Swt. The ♀ is a truly black butterfly, as the yellow median bands are absent and the submarg. spots are reduced. That leaves the blue band of the HW (which is larger than in ♂) striking-ly set against the black wings.
Habitat.   Scorns the domestic surroundings preferred by its eastern relative the Black Swt. Upper Sonoran Zone of the more arid mountain ranges, but hilltops to at least 11,500 ft.

Flight. May into September. At least two-brooded; in Colo. produces small spring brood and a larger one in late July-August. Broods relate to amount of rainfall.

Food Plant. Green sage (*Artemisia dracunculus*). This is the wild version of the delectable herb, tarragon. Larvae can be hand raised on fennel, which has similar taste and odor, though unrelated.

Early Stages. The eggs, larvae and pupae are larger than those of eastern Black Swt., despite the fact that adults are of similar size. Eggs pale green; mature larva green with black bands and orange spots; but some are almost all black, which may be the result of cool weather, as Steven Sims reports that nearly black larvae of *P. zelicaon* can be produced by raising them at 20°C (68°F) (private communication).

Forms. The insect described is the typical or black form of the species: *P. bairdii* f. "bairdii"; it is not a subspecies as it and the two yellow forms can come from the same parents. If *P. oregonius* (6) is not a species it will have a place here as a subspecies; it flies in a geographically separate area and has no dark form; all offspring are similar yellow butterflies. Elsewhere there are two yellow forms which fly with the black ones in some areas, or completely dominate in other regions.

P. bairdii f. "brucei" Edwards 1895   Pl. II, Fig. 3.

Broad yellow median band and narrow black inner border on UpHW, which sometimes crosses base of cell. It is larger than *P. zelicaon* (8) with which it sometimes flies. The best distinction is the abdomen which in "brucei" is yellow on sides and underneath, but with two black lines running along each lower side. (In *P. zelicaon* the abdomen is black with a yellow side stripe; in *P. oregonius* abdomen is yellow with a black stripe along back and a narrow black line along mid underside.) Anal eye spot of "brucei" is different: small, and only forepart orange; margin short and cuts obliquely to pupil. (Specimen in Pl. II is atypical in not having pupil tied to margin; females flying with this male were normal.) In *P. zelicaon* pupil is free and centered; in *P. oregonius* it is to rear of eye spot, bulbous and tied with horizontal bar. In a series "brucei" will show the basal half of UnFW cells as black, while *P. oregonius* and *P. machaon* have this area washed with yellow.

51

P. bairdii f. "hollandii" Edwards 1892   Not figured

The median bands of both wings broader than in typical or black f. "bairdii" and there is more black at the base of UpHW than in f. "brucei". The edge of the median band often fades into the black with mixed scales of each color.

Distribution.

Canada: f. "brucei" at Beulah in Manitoba; at Eastend, Val Marie, Big Muddy, Claybank and Crooked Lake in Saskatchewan; and Alberta.

N. Dakota: f. "brucei" in Badlands.

Neb.: Four old records for Sioux Co. in nw. corner; Johnson's list does not include it as a Neb. species, but Kohler has collected, "brucei" in w. Neb.

Kansas: Field reports that all three forms have been taken in Scott Co. of w. Kan. (Black Swt. also recorded for this county.)

Okla.: f. "brucei" possible (no records) in Panhandle, as it flies in adjoining Baca Co. of se. Colorado.

Wyo.: f. "brucei" in Johnson and Teton Cos., but rare. Old records for Albany Co.; possible in Carbon and Converse Cos. These are all f. "brucei". The eastern Black Swt. also flies in these last three counties.

Colo.: The Arkansas River area on e. slope, from Cañon City W to Salida and Buena Vista, S to the San Luis Valley. All three forms in this area. The f. "brucei" from Baca Co. in se. corner. Typical form (only) in Mesa Verde, but f. "hollandii" found in Montezuma Co. Typical form extends N to w. central Colo. in Mesa Co. Both typical and "brucei" in Delta Co., and N and W to the Blue Mt. Plateau around Dinosaur Nat'l Mon. In Moffat Co. the yellow form is said to be an intergrade between "brucei" and *P. oregonius* (6).

New Mexico: Records scanty. Reported as uncommon in Manzano Mts., Mt. Taylor, Ladron Peak, and San Mateo Mts. The situation in Sangre de Cristo Mts. (s. extension of Rocky Mts.) unknown. It would be expected in mts. of nw. corner of state.

Arizona: Flies on both sides of Grand Canyon; Flagstaff; Wupatki Nat'l Mon. Mts. of Mogollon Rim across central Ariz., W to Mingus Mt. which is S of Jerome in Yavapai Co. Could fly in mts. on e. border of state, but no records.

Utah: Typical form tends to be rare and f. "brucei" common, becoming increasingly dominant from south to north. Along s.

border in e. Washington, Kane and San Juan Cos., N through Sevier and Carbon Cos. Uintah Basin in NE (Harper's Corner). West of Salt Lake City in Stansbury Mts., Tooele County.

Nevada: Both typical form and "brucei" fly in the Toiyabe Range, Lander and Nye Cos. Since this range is near center of the state they may also fly in other isolated ranges.

Calif.: Localized in the San Bernardino Mts. in county of that name; breeds from 6000 to 9000 ft. Specific locales: Barton Flats, Camp Redford, Jenks Lake, Poopout Hill, and Onyx at e. end of mts. The typical form dominates with 1%-4% "brucei", and "hollandii" much scarcer than that.

Baja California: Hoffmann lists it for n. Baja and n. Sonora (?); checking that would be a good project.

Note. There is an undescribed population referred to as the Badlands Swallowtail. In North Dakota at least this is just f. "brucei"; it is double-brooded and the larval food plant is green sage.

6. *Papilio oregonius* Edwards 1876

OREGON SWALLOWTAIL Pl. II, Fig. 5.

Expanse: 65-85 mm **Tails:** 8-11 mm

Description. Another yellow-median-banded Swallowtail, resembling the Anise Swt. (8) with which it flies. The Anise Swt. is smaller, has a black abdomen, and the pupil of its eye spot is centered. The Alaskan Swt. (1) is similar but has no pupil at all in eye spot. The Oregon Swt. differs from "brucei" (5) in range and, in addition to the points listed under that form, by having less black toward outer margin of UnFW.

Habitat. A butterfly of the arid sagebrush country of eastern Washington and Oregon, though it likes water courses and is also at home in towns of the area. Adults attracted to thistle bloom and garden flowers.

Flight. Double-brooded; one flight in June-July, the other Aug.-Sept.

Food Plant. Green sage (*Artemisia dracunculus*) of family Compositae. Can be raised on fennel, but in nature does not use the Parsley family.

Early Stages. Mature larva light green, with black segmental bands interrupted by six yellow spots.

Distribution.
Canada: southern interior of B.C. to U.S. (Wash.) border.

Wash.: E of Cascades along e. edge of state from Metaline Falls to Clarkston. Okanogan Highlands and Columbia Basin. Specifically: Brewster, Pateros, Grand Coulee, Chelan, Priest Rapids, and Lind.

Oregon: Also E of Cascades; in n. tier of cos.: Wasco, Sherman, Gilliam, Morrow, Umatilla; in c. Ore., Jefferson Co.; on e. border, in Baker Co. Perkins (1968) says more southerly records not verified (in Deschutes and Klamath Cos.).

Note. Status not proven, but whether species or subspecies all the particulars will be the same.

7. *Papilio joanae* Heitzman 1973

JOAN'S SWALLOWTAIL
(For Fig. see *Jour. of Res. on Lepid.*, Vol. 12, #1, p. 4)

Expanse. FW length 44-54 mm.

Description. Male darker than *P. bairdii* ♂ (5), while ♀ is as dark above but lighter below. Joan's Swt. has very orange spots in median band on under side. Differs from Black Swt. by: having apical spot of median band of UpFW single and small (in Black Swt. this spot is usually divided by a round black dot); pupil of eye spot in *joanae* touches inner margin of spot; greatest difference said to be in habitat, food plants, and larvae.

Habitat. A forest species; the Black Swt. flies in same general area, but in open places and along roads, while Joan's Swt. confines itself to the woods. If it proves to be a species it will have arrived either by the route of ecological isolation, or by geographical isolation elsewhere and a shift to present area.

Flight. Two broods: one April-June, and second Aug. and early Sept.

Food Plants. Meadow parsnip (*Thaspium barbinode*); *Taenidia integerrima*; both in Parsley family.

Early Stages. Description not yet published, but from pictures the mature larva has the black bands much fragmented.

Distribution. Type locality is Warsaw, Benton Co., Missouri; also taken in Camden, Carter, Franklin, Johnson, Maries, St. Louis and Washington Cos., all of which are in cs. Missouri. Also in Knox Co.

Note. This species is too new for certain status, but falls between the eastern Black and Baird's Swallowtails.

8.   *Papilio zelicaon*   Lucas 1852

ANISE SWALLOWTAIL

Pl. II, Fig. 4.

Expanse: 63-73 mm   **Tails:** 7-9 mm

Description. Sexes similar. Another yellow-median-banded Swt. with markings very similar to those of the Alaskan Swt., *P. machaon* (1). The Anise Swt. has a black abdomen with a yellow side stripe, a black pupil in center of eye spot, and a black discal cell in UnFW with two yellow bars in it. The Anise Swt. is distinguished from either the Oregon Swt. (6) or f. "brucei" (5) by the black abdomen and smaller wing expanse.

Habitat. There are three divisions. Some populations cling to their native food plants and remain in rugged country at any elevation, from sea level to 13,000 ft. A second group has shifted to garden fennel, which grows wild along roads and on vacant lots; these like city parks and gardens as well as open country, and as fennel stays green all summer they have more than one brood. A third segment of the species contingent has switched to *Citrus* for a food plant and lives in cultivated orange and lemon groves. The combination gives this species access to nearly all available environments within its range.

Flight. In coastal San Diego Co., Calif., it flies in all months of the year; in n. Calif., March for first emergence, through Sept.; same in Ore. In Wyo., May to July.

Food Plants. Various members of the Parsley family, esp. the genus *Lomatium*, biscuitroot, for native food plants. In n. Calif., *Lomatium dasycarpum* and *L. utriculatum*; in s. Calif., those plus *L. dissectum* var. *multifidum*. In Utah, *L. grayi*;in Colo., *L. parryi* and also *Harbouria trachypleura*. In Wyo. on *Pseudocymopterus montanus*. In Calif., also on *Oenanthe sarmentosa* and *Heracleum maximum*. The name Anise Swt. is based on the fact that, in the West, fennel that grows wild is often called "wild Anise" although it is little like *Pimpinella anisum* (anise) except for taste. In addition to these, and doubtless other, Umbelliferae, this butterfly also utilizes citrus of the Rue Family.

Early Stages. Mature larva green, with orange- or yellow-spotted black transverse bands. Consumes the flower buds and flowers as well as tender leaf growth.

Distribution and Subspecies.
There are two nearly identical subspecies:

8.a.   *Papilio zelicaon zelicaon*

As described above.

8.b.   *P. z. gothica*   Remington 1968

These two look so much alike that it is best to depend on distribution for separation determination. In *gothica*, color differs with the sex, ♂♂ being mustard yellow, and ♀♀ straw yellow; it also has two yellow lines along forward edge of UpFW, about 2/3 of distance out from base. Other differences are given in Remington (1968). Shapiro (1975) has shown that the early spring brood of lowland Calif. *z. zelicaon* resembles *z. gothica* in the characters used by Remington to differentiate the Rocky Mtn. subsp.

Canada: throughout B.C., s. Alberta. Race *gothica* (above) in s. Sask.

N. Dakota: Badlands.

Wyo.: the subsp. *gothica*, in moist meadows, recorded from w. tier of cos., Yellowstone Park, Teton, Sublette, and Lincoln Cos.; E of continental divide, Sheridan Co. in N; in Carbon, Albany and Converse Cos. in SE.

Neb.: Pine Ridge area of NW, spreading east—recorded from Paxton, Keith Co.

(Not recorded for Kansas.)

Colo.: subspecies *gothica* flies on both e. and w. slopes of Rocky Mts.; town of Gothic, Gunnison Co., alt. 9500 ft, is type locality.

New Mexico: higher mts.; common on Mt. Taylor, and uncommon in Sandia and Manzano Mts.

Utah: largely in w. counties: mts. of Cache, Rich, and Weber Cos. Wasatch Mts.; Stansbury Mts. of Tooele Co., and the ranges S from there; also Henry Mts. in e. Garfield Co.

Ariz.: possibly along n. border; elsewhere it is replaced by other species of this group.

Wash.: on both sides of Cascade Mts.; in E it flies together with *P. oregonius* (6) in places like Brewster, Okanogan Co., and Soap Lake, Grant Co.; on w. side of mts., in Seattle, Mt. Rainier, etc.

Ore.: most of state, except that records for actual coast counties seem to be lacking, as they are for Malheur Co. in SE.

Idaho: scattered records in mts.

Nev.: scattered records: Reno; Ruby Mts. of e. Nev.; Toiyabe Range, Nye and Lander Cos. of c. Nevada.

Calif.: all of state except se. deserts; islands off s. coast.

Baja Calif.: there are records for both Baja and n. Sonora, but these should be checked to see where Rudkin's Swt. fits.

9. *Papilio nitra* Edwards 1884

NITRA SWALLOWTAIL   Pl. III, Fig. 2.

Expanse: 60-75 mm   **Tails:** 6-7 mm

Description. Sexes sometimes differ. ♂: ground color black with median bands and submarg. spots of yellow; inner margin of median band not sharply defined, as black scales are peppered out onto yellow. UpFW: a minute black dot in uppermost triangular spot of median band; a distinct yellow bar at apex of cell, and usually a second bar faintly indicated below first. UpHW: broad black base covering half or more of cell; spots of median band well separated by black. Between median band and submarg. band is a row of blue marks. Anteriormost submarg. spot faintly washed with rufous (not indicated on plate). Abdomen: a single row of light yellow dots, or dashes, along middle of each side. ♀: type specimen was male-like; 2nd form has increased black, and black dusting on FW; HW has completely black cell, and median band is reduced to a narrow, curving row of yellow spots.

P. nitra can be distinguished from all forms of *P. bairdii* (5) by centered pupil in the eye spot, from *P. polyxenes* (2) and *P. indra* (11) by the single but complete row of lateral abdominal spots (*polyxenes* has at least a double row on each side; *indra* has only a single bar at tip of abdomen, or no spots).

Habitat. Definitely montane. A Montana lepidopterist points out that part of *nitra's* rarity lies in the fact that it flies above 6000 ft, in May, and few roads are open through the snowy passes at that time. In Alberta, occurs in foothills.

Flight. May and June.

Food Plant. *Harbouria trachypleura* in Colorado.

Early Stages. Apparently resemble those of Anise Swt.

Distribution.

Canada: Southern Alberta from U.S. border to Nordegg; most common 30 miles W of Calgary.

Montana: Type locality, Judith Mts., in ec. part of state. Steven Kohler has collected it in Garnett Mts., near Hoover Creek, Powell Co., W of continental divide. There is a specimen in U. of Mont. collection from sw. part of state.

Wyo.: According to Ferris (1971), *P. nitra* flies in moist meadows of Canadian Life Zone, 8000 to 10,000 ft, in Park Co. in nw. and Crook Co. in ne. corner of state. Converse and Albany Cos. in SE; in Albany Co. it has been taken in the Laramie Mts. E of Laramie, and W of Laramie around Centennial and up the pass into the lower Snowy Range.

Neb.: One specimen from w. Neb., Bull Canyon, near Harrisburg, Banner Co., 2 June 1919.

Colo.: Restricted to the Front Range, E of the continental divide, from Larimer Co. S to Douglas Co. (Jarre Canyon), and concentrated in the foothills W of Denver and N to the Boulder area, from 6000 to 8000 ft. As yet unknown from W of the divide.

Note. There is both debate and study of this presumed species. Remington crossed specimens of the eastern Black Swt. with the Anise Swallowtail and got specimens resembling *P. nitra*, although different. For a time this promoted the view that *nitra* might be a hybrid. Hooper (1973) reported that larvae from Eston, wc. Sask., found on garden dill, produced several *P. z. gothica* and one "nitra". A similar report comes from James Oberfoell of North Dakota, who raised larvae found on garden dill in the sw. corner of N.D. The group produced adults which were two-thirds *zelicaon* and one-third *nitra*-like black swallowtails. In Colorado Michael Fisher has been working on a scientific project for mass rearing of larvae from *P. z. gothica* and *P. nitra*. When it is completed the relationships will be worked out and these will mean changed distributions and possibly changed names.

10. *Papilio rudkini* Comstock 1935

RUDKIN'S SWALLOWTAIL Pl. II, Fig. 6.

Expanse: 65-70+ mm **Tails:** 6-8 mm

Description. Since there are three very different forms, it is impossible to generalize, but the typical form is similar to the Anise Swt. (8). Its range, however, is separate except for a slight overlap on the

w. edge of the Calif. deserts. One of the best distinctions is that the yellow submarginal spots of UpFW are rounded and far apart. [In *P. zelicaon* (8) these are linear in shape and tend to form a band.] Comstock pointed out in the original descr. that the spots of the median band tend to be rounded on their outer edges (see Pl. II, Fig. 6). This is a useful distinction, as in *P. oregonius* (6) the outer edge is concave, while in f. "brucei" and *P. zelicaon* it is straight. The black marginal band of UpHW is broader in *P. rudkini* than in *P. zelicaon*.

Habitat. Lower Sonoran desert washes and canyons of the desert mts. Specially adapted to arid climate; pupae may delay emergence as much as 4 to 6 years; thus the species is able to respond with a mass emergence after a favorable rainfall which starts food plant growth. Type locality: Ivanpah Mts., San Bernardino Co., Calif.

Flight. Feb. to Oct. Double-brooded, but emergence of second brood variable to suit favorable weather.

Food Plants. Turpentine-broom (*Thamnosma montana*), of Rue family. Under competition, switches at times to *Cymopterus panamintensis* var. *acutifolia*, of Parsley family. In Yuma, Ariz., reported on wild carrot (*Daucus carota*), also an umbellifer.

Early Stages. Mature larvae variable, independently of adult variation. Some larvae are nearly all black with green streaks, but these don't necessarily produce the dark adult form. Some larvae are almost all green, or even white.

Distribution.

Calif.: Desert SE; desert e. half of San Diego Co: Scissors Crossing; Imperial Co.; e. 3/4 of Riverside Co., including Joshua Tree Nat'l Mon.; San Bernardino Co. from e. edge of mts. and N through Victorville to the Death Valley area.

Ariz.: All of w. Ariz. S of Mogollon Rim, as far E as Stewart Mt. Dam E of Phoenix, and Oracle N of Tucson; distribution also follows food plants up Colorado R. and bottom of Grand Canyon, emerging again in the Painted Desert area, flying at least as far E as Tuba City.

Nev.: Presumably lower tip of state and lower Virgin River.

Utah: Intrusions up the Virgin R. from Nev. and Ariz. to St. George, Utah; southern slope of Beaver Dam Mts; this is typical form, as dark form is rare here.

Mexico: Possibly n. Sonora and n. Baja Calif.

Forms. The typical form of *P. rudkini* is described above. Variants are:

f. "clarki" Chermock & Chermock 1937

A dark form in which male resembles Baird's Swt. but has paler undersurface. Yellow median band of UpHW set in further and occupying more of cell. ♀ differs from ♀ of Baird's Swt. by having a faint median band. This form rare in Calif., except in Providence Mts., where it may form 25% of population. At Yuma, Ariz., this form and the typical are 50%/50%.

f. "comstocki" Chermock & Chermock 1937

A yellow form but with wider black margin than the typical form, and with considerable blue between median and submarg. bands on UpHW. Also more black at base of HW, so median band is narrower. Hand-mated crosses between the Anise Swt. and Rudkin's Swt. can produce individuals similar to this form, but that is no proof that it happens in nature.

Note. This is another "species" of most uncertain status. Comstock described *rudkini* as a subspecies of Baird's Swt. Remington (1968) thought it nearer to *P. zelicaon*, while present s. California students either grant it species status or relate it to the eastern Black Swallowtail (2) of Arizona. Obviously it will become a prime subject for genetic studies.

11. *Papilio indra* Reakirt 1866

INDRA SWALLOWTAIL   Pl. III, Fig. 3.

Expanse: 60-70 mm   **Tails:** variable, from tooth of 2 mm to tail 6 mm

Description. Sexes similar. Black or brownish black; median bands and submarginal spots creamy yellow; submarg. spots of forewing rounded and well separated; those of HW somewhat lunulate. Median band variable in width, but in typical subspecies approx. that of ♂ Black Swt. (2). On UpFW there is an extra, rounded, cream dot set inward from apex of median band; at apex of cell there is a curved cream line, or sometimes two, thus: ( ). On UpHW spots of median band are joined together, often passing just through outer end of cell. The blue spots in row between band and submarg. spots are larger in ♀. Anal eye spot orange, with incomplete black margin and a centered dot of black.

Habitat. Mountain or foothill country where there is an abundance of brush and boulders; these are serpentine rocks in w. Calif., and granite in Sierra Nevada. Not particular as to altitude: Hopfinger reported it flying in sagebrush-greasewood at the confluence of the Okanogan and Columbia Rivers in Wash. state at 580 ft. In the sw. limit of its range, in Napa Co., Calif., it flies at 1200 ft. In the Sierra Nevada it flies at 9000 ft or more.

Flight. April-May in Napa Co., and June to early July in Sierra Nevada of Calif. May through July, and perhaps Aug., in Wash. state.

Food Plants. Members of Parsley family (Umbelliferae). In Shasta Co. and Sierra Nevada in Calif., *Pteryxia terebinthina*; also reported on *P. petraea* in some places. In Napa Co., Calif., on *Lomatium marginatum*, and, at s. end of Calif. range, on *Tauschia parishii*. In Utah on *Lomatium parryi*; in Colo. on *L. simplex* and *Harbouria trachypleura*.

Early Stages. Mature larva black with pinkish or yellowish bands over forepart of each segment; spots on these bands golden yellow.

Distribution and Subspecies. There are seven subspecies.

11.a.   *P. indra indra*

·As described above.

Distribution.

> Wash.: Brewster, Camp Gilbert, and Cooney Lake, Okanogan Co.; Leavenworth, Chelan Co.; Hanford, Benton Co.; Pomeroy, Garfield Co.; Sheep Lake, Yakima Co. In general, e. slopes of Cascades, Okanogan Highlands, Columbia Basin, and Blue Mts.
>
> Idaho: Custer Co.
>
> Oregon: E of Cascades in n. tier of Cos.: Wasco, Jefferson, Gilliam, Umatilla, and Wallowa; along e. border of state in Grant and Baker Cos.; possibly Jackson Co. in S.
>
> Calif.: Starting in N: 10 mi. NE of Weed, Siskiyou Co.; Shasta L., Shasta Co.; coming SW: e. Mendocino Co. and Lake Co., to Coast Range of Napa Co. W of Lake Berryessa. On e. side of state there is a species gap between Shasta Co. and the higher mts. of Placer Co., from there along high Sierra Nevada to Fresno and Tulare Cos.; isolated record at Piute Peak, Kern Co., at 8000 ft; on e. slope of Sierra Nevada in Mono and Inyo Cos.; also in the detached White Mts. of those counties.
>
> Wyo.: Transition Zone of Lincoln and Teton Cos.; in SE in Platte, Albany and Converse Cos.
>
> Neb.: Two old records from Pine Ridge and Wildcat Range in w. part of state.

Colo.: Front Range from Larimer Co. S to the S. Platte River in Jefferson Co. This subspecies does not occur W of continental divide.

Utah: One record: South Willow Creek, Stansbury Range, Tooele Co.

11.b. *Papilio indra pergamus* Hy Edwards 1874

EDWARDS' SWALLOWTAIL   Pl. III, Fig. 6.

Expanse: 70-80 mm   **Tails:** 7 mm

Description. Like *indra indra* except for the tail, which is narrow to base. FW is typically proportionately narrower and more angular.

Flight. From end of March to end of June.

Food Plants. *Tauschia arguta* and *T. parishii.* Also the biscuit root (*Lomatium lucidum*), all in Parsley family.

Early Stages. In mature larva the black ground color is reduced to patches; extensive white bands with yellow spots; head a deep yellow with black streaks.

Distribution. Calif.: Santa Barbara: Larvae should not be collected from this weak colony. Los Angeles Co.: San Gabriel Mts.: Camp Rincon, S.G. Canyon. San Bernardino Co.: s. slope of San Bernardino Mts. Riverside Co.: Idyllwild in San Jacinto Mts. San Diego Co.: Laguna Mts.: Monument Peak, Garnet Pk., Mt. Laguna.

11.c. *Papilio indra minori* Cross 1936

MINOR'S SWALLOWTAIL

Expanse: 70-80+ mm   **Tails:** 7 mm

Description. UpFW: median band much narrowed, spots a third or less the size of those on *P. indra indra.* On UpHW band even more reduced, being widest on forward edge and a mere line over anal eye spot. Blue band between median and submarg. marks highly developed and wide even in ♂.

Flight. From mid-May to early June in Colo. Sometimes there is a second partial brood for which there are no food plants; larva identical with next subsp.

Food Plant. *Lomatium eastwoodae* and possibly *L. grayi.*

Distribution.

W. Colo. and se. Utah.

Colo.: Mesa and Delta Cos.; Black Canyon of Gunnison Nat'l Mon., Montrose Co.; Mesa Verde Nat'l Park, Montezuma Co. Utah: Moab, Grand Co.; Abajo Mts., San Juan Co. (July). New Mexico: one record, Los Alamos Co.

11.d. *Papilio indra kaibabensis* Bauer 1955

GRAND CANYON SWALLOWTAIL

Expanse: ♂ 76 mm, ♀ 86 mm   **Tails:** 10 mm

Description. A large, essentially black and blue Swt., the most elegantly beautiful race of this species. Jet black, with median band greatly reduced or absent; submarginal spots small and clouded black, those between tail and eye spot absent. Pupil of eye spot large, leaving only a rim of fulvous orange.

Habitat: This subspecies inhabits the inner cliffs of the Grand Canyon, but also flies above, on the North Rim, which is 9000 ft, and on the floor of the canyon.

Flight. Above rim: Point Imperial, Cape Royal, Bright Angel Point, all on North Rim, and at Ryan Ranger Station, Kaibab Plateau on n. side. Also at Yavapai Point, South Rim. All in Arizona. The first brood hatches from late May to early July, and there is a second brood in August.

Food Plant. *Pteryxia petraea* of Parsley family.

Early Stages. Mature larva is deep black with six orange spots on each segment; from spots to forward edge of segment is a pink band. This larva is identical with that of *P. indra minori*, but the pupa is a light tannish pink, while that of *minori* is gray-tan or brown-tan.

Distribution. Breeds half-way between floor and north rim of Grand Canyon, at Roaring Springs, at 4000 ft.

11.e. *Papilio indra fordi* Comstock & Martin 1956

FORD'S SWALLOWTAIL   Pl. III, Fig. 4.

Expanse: 55-62 mm   **Tails:** 4-5 mm

Description. The smallest race. Spots and bands are yellow to light cream; marginal fringe spots more prominent than in typical subspecies; median bands much broader. UpHW median band triangular—broad on forward edge of wing and reducing to a point over eye spot.

Flight. In late March and early April, among the boulders of barren mountains in the Mojave Desert, Calif.

Food Plants. Larvae feed on *Cymopterus panamintensis*, of Parsley family. If that is unavailable they switch to turpentine broom, *Thamnosma montana* of Rue family.

Early Stages. The mature larva is black with an inverted orange V on the head, and with white bands on each segment encompassing four large lemon yellow spots.

Distribution.

Calif.: Granite, Sheephole, Coxcomb, Eagle and Calico Mts. of the Mojave Desert, San Bernardino Co.

Nevada: Northwestern Colorado Desert.

11.f. *Papilio indra martini* Emmel & Emmel 1966

MARTIN'S SWALLOWTAIL

Expanse: 66-72 mm **Tails:** 6 mm

Description. Dull black with cream markings; all spots clouded with black on edges. UpHW median band narrower than in *P. indra indra*; it skirts end of cell then bends inward in a narrow line. Pupil of eye spot large.

Flight. April through May, with small second brood, June-July.

Food Plant. *Lomatium parryi.*

Early Stages. Mature larva is black with *pink* bands, with a white dot at bottom of each band, a white patch on each proleg.

Distribution. South Fork of Bonanza King Mine Canyon, Gilroy Canyon, Mitchell Caverns State Park area, all in Providence Mts., San Bernardino Co., Calif.

11.g. *Papilio indra nevadensis* Emmel & Emmel 1971

NEVADA SWALLOWTAIL Pl. III, Fig. 5.

Expanse: 65-73 mm **Tails:** 4.8-7.5 mm

Description. Differs from *indra indra* and *i. pergamus* by having broader median bands on both wings, but esp. on FW.; these markings even broader on under side.

Flight. In canyons of arid mountain ranges, with two broods: a strong flight in May, and a weaker one in August.

Food Plant. *Pteryxia petraea* of Parsley family.

Early Stages. Larvae have two forms: black with pink-tinted, cream-colored transverse bands which end at level of spiracles on thoracic segments, and below that level on abdomen. In a second form, bands on head and thorax are absent while those on abdomen are much reduced.

Distribution. Nevada: In canyons: Jett, Kingston, Peavine Creek, Summit, and Twin River; these are along east side of Toiyabe Range in Nye and Lander Cos., central Nevada. Also in the Toquima Range, Nye Co.

Note. There are other atypical *indra* populations: one in Pershing Co., N of above area, one in Spring Mts., Clark Co., far to the SE, and another in Pine Valley Mts. of Washington Co. in the sw. corner of Utah.

65

4

SOME HOWS AND WHYS OF SPECIES

Now that the reader has become acquainted with what is probably the most difficult group of Swallowtails, he is likely to have been left with a question or two in the back of his mind. One of these may be: Why are there so many visually nearly identical species in North America? Why not just one or two of these species? A question which follows would be to inquire about what a species is, and how one tells whether a certain butterfly is a species or a subspecies. In every way the American branch of the Old World Swallowtail group is ideal for studying these questions, since its members are recent species, relatively speaking, or are still in the process of speciation. Being in the process leads to uncertainty, since there is no qualitative difference between distinctions which separate species and those which separate subspecies. No one, for instance, is positive that Rudkin's Swallowtail has actually become a separate species, although everyone will grant that it is an independent population, and the same is true for several other members of this group.

These problem entities bring up the question: What is a species, and how does one find out? The answer is somewhat historical, as there are three ways to tell a species, the oldest method based simply on form, while the newer two are based on observation of the organism in relation to its home environment, and on genetic studies. Ideally, all three of these approaches should be brought into play, but most insects were described originally from dead specimens which had been sent to a museum. All that the describer had to go on were such things as wing pattern, venation, size of palps, the presence or absence of pits or spines, the parts of the genitalia, or any other item which could be described to differentiate one insect from another.

In general, classification by noting differences and similarities works quite well, for the good reason that these visible distinctions are based on genetic differences, and we will come to the value of these shortly. When classification by form is backed up with observations in the field it is much strengthened, since one can then see that insect A, though it looks much like B, flies together with B without interbreeding, prefers higher elevations in general, emerges one month later, and in other ways behaves separately. Form alone has no such tempering and determination is likely to be arbitrary. Until recently the British Museum (Natural History) had classified the Anise Swallowtail as a subspecies of the Old World Swallowtail, because the main *visible* difference between the two is the presence of a "pupil" in the anal eye spot of the Anise Swt., and that was thought to be too small a difference for granting species status. American students who had observed both butterflies in the field had always considered the two to be separate species, and genetic studies have proven this view correct.

The third approach for determining species is based on genetics, and this is necessarily recent. While genetic studies at a technical level can be complicated, they also have a practical side, in which even a relative beginner can participate by way of hybridizing or crossing presumed species. The first thing one needs to know is the contemporary definition of a species. No one has contrived a perfect definition which fits all plants and animals alike, but the following will do for sexually reproducing animals, including butterflies:

> "Species are groups of actually or potentially interbreeding natural populations, which are reproductively isolated from other such groups."   (Mayr)

It follows from this definition that if two kinds of butterflies are of different species they will be unable to interbreed (usually), even though they may produce first-generation hybrids; and one can test this possibility by hand crossing them under controlled conditions in the laboratory, or even in one's home.

There is a "why" which can be answered at this point: Why do new species come into being? Perhaps the question can be rephrased, in light of the definition, to read: How does reproductive isolation come about? So long as any population continues to interbreed there will be a gene flow back and forth between its members and they will all share a common genetic make-up. However, small genetic changes are continual and if one segment of the population is cut off from the remainder it will in time become at least partially isolated in a genetic as well as in a geographical sense. If this situation continues, the isolated population then becomes a subspecies, through accumulation of unshared genetic changes. Present thinking holds that subspecies arise because of such geographic isolation, perhaps reinforced by habitat differences. Since separate geographical areas present different conditions, selection and adaptation will follow a different course in each, and since all of the accumulating differences are controlled by genes, the pattern of these differences will also shift. If and when the accumulated genetic changes become great enough the two populations will become reproductively incompatible. At that point the former subspecies becomes a full species.

Another "why" can be answered here: Why do the species of the Old World Swallowtail group look so much alike? The reason is that most of them are derived from the break-up of one or two species, which has taken place in comparatively recent times, and is in fact continuing at the present time. If this break-up had taken place in the more distant past some of these species might have become extinct, and that would have produced wider gaps between the remaining ones, just as the gap between Indra and the rest of the Old World Swallowtail group is wider.

A "how" question arises at this point: How does the geographical isolation of some part of the species population come about? A common way takes the form of a gradual expansion outward from the point of origin. This all-inclusive spread can be seen in the Old World Swallowtail itself, which is found in a nearly complete band around the earth in the northern hemisphere, with one end of it in England and the other in eastern Canada. But isolation can also occur with little actual movement by the population. We know that at some time in the Pliocene the Sierra Nevada/Cascade mountain chain was thrust up in the far west of the U.S., creating a barrier to rain storms traveling in from the Pacific Ocean. In the region east of the mountains, which had once been well watered, an arid basin area was created, with great deserts to the south. There is no fossil butterfly record from those times, but one can see that populations would be separated and that some of these would face very different conditions.

The ice ages of the Pleistocene, which began approximately one million years ago, were in the nature of warm and cold pulsations. Early in the epoch northwestern North America enjoyed a warm temperate climate, with palm trees and cycads growing in what is now Alaska; but during the glacial periods ice covered Canada and at times parts of the western and northeastern United States. During these icy periods members of this Old World group of swallowtails were forced southwestward or southeastward. When warmer periods ensued those that were adapted to cold would take refuge in the higher elevations where the cold lingers, or migrate northward. The effect of these temperature fluctuations and consequent movements of butterfly populations was to disrupt broad gene flow and produce isolated populations. The Indra Swallowtail, for example, now has isolated populations in the Rocky Mts. of Colorado, the Sierra Nevada and desert ranges of California, and other regions mentioned in the preceding chapter.

Climatic changes assault a species from without, while other pressures develop from within. The immense potential of a single pair of breeding butterflies has been mentioned, and also the fact that predators, adverse weather and other influences tend to keep a population stable, which means the replacement of one pair with only one other pair each season. In some years, however, a population will "luck-out" and there will be an increase or even an explosion in numbers and, since the parent population was stabilized near the level that the locale will support, the surplus must try to push elsewhere. The eastern Black Swallowtail obviously originated in the north, along with its fellow species, but now has extended its range into northwestern South America.

Two English geneticists have studied the Old World Swallowtail group by interbreeding different species, and they make a point indicating that the Alaskan Swallowtail reached its present area in a push outward from Asia. Needless to say, these radiations are not events of one year, or of a hundred, but the result of continuous surplus-population pressure. Clarke & Sheppard (1956) state:

"Most of the N. American members of the *machaon* group were apparently present in America and isolated from the

Asiatic forms during the ice age. However, *P. machaon aliaska*, appears not to be one of these but to be the result of an invasion from Asia after the ice age."

If their surmise is correct it means that the related populations previously here had retreated south and, after the final ice age, the far north was left open and unclaimed until the Alaskan subspecies arrived from across Bering Strait.

The reasoning of the two geneticists is based on the form of the "eye spot" and its border. In European and Asian subspecies of the Old World Swallowtail the eye spot is "blind"—without a "pupil"—while the upper margin often consists of a single black line. In related American species, on the other hand, the eye spot has a pupil, and above the bright eye are double black lines with a blue band between them. Thus one sees that even geneticists rely upon the evidence presented by form.

Having given some account of how reproductive isolation grows out of geographic isolation, we now address the important question of how one tells when a subspecies has changed its status to that of a full species. Reproductive isolation is not entirely a matter of genetic incompatibility, since in nature two species may be kept apart by such things as courtship behavior, or breeding seasons which come at different times. Among frogs the separation is by voice. For species status, all that is required is that the two populations not interbreed when they come together *in nature*. Under artificial conditions some valid species are perfectly interfertile, notable examples being ducks of the family Anatidae. In mammals of the genus *Canis*, and mice of the genus *Peromyscus*, there are sympatric species that are fertile when crossed under laboratory conditions, but do not cross in nature.

However, a growing genetic isolation is to be expected as a species begins its evolutionary digression, and students of butterfly speciation are favored over those who study birds and mammals in that they can actually test the degree of genetic isolation in rather easily managed experiments. The method is to hand-cross members of populations which may or may not be separate species. When the cross is between *distant* relatives there will be no result at all. When the Indra Swallowtail was crossed with the eastern Black Swallowtail the eggs laid showed fertilization color changes, but only two showed larval development, and the one which hatched produced a caterpillar which died within two hours. That result had been expected, as Indra is the only member of the group with distinctively different genitalia, and hence presumed greater genetic distance from other species.

When judging species status as purely a matter of genetic isolation, two standards seem to be in current use. The more rigorous of these might read: "Males of one group are cross-bred with females of another, and also the reverse. If they are of separate species, the offspring of these matings will be infertile when again cross-bred in the same manner with the parent species." There is no doubt that if back crosses to the parent species are infertile it indicates a high degree of genetic isolation; but if that were accepted as the only criterion of species status it would controvert some known facts.

For example, experimental crossings have been made between species in the Tiger Swallowtail group, which is discussed in the next chapter. Several species in this group are very closely related; they will hybridize readily when hand mated in captivity; and the offspring of these matings are fertile when back crossed. Both the Western Tiger Swallowtail, *P. rutulus* (13), and the equally western Pale Swallowtail, *P. eurymedon* (15), hand cross readily with the Eastern Tiger Swallowtail, *P. glaucus* (12). If the offspring of such matings are back crossed to the parent species, *P. glaucus*, the offspring of this following generation are fertile (Clarke & Sheppard 1957). If we held to the definition given in the preceding paragraph all three of the species would have to be considered subspecies, since they are not sterile in a back cross. However, in reality (in nature) this is not so. The Pale Swallowtail and the Western Tiger fly together throughout much of the West without ever hybridizing, despite ample opportunity, so they are known to be distinct species.

A less rigorous definition of a species, from a purely genetic viewpoint, would be that if the first-generation hybrids are sterile when mated with one another, then there is enough genetic difference between the parent populations to warrant species status. Clarke and Sheppard (1955) made extensive crosses within the Old World Swallowtail group, between: Black Swt. (2) X Alaskan (1); Short-tailed (4) X Alaskan (1); Short-tailed (4) X Black Swt. (2); Anise Swt. (8) X Alaskan (1); Black Swt. (2) X Anise Swt. (8); Short-tailed (4) X Anise Swallowtail (8). These species are genetically near enough to one another to produce a first generation, but the results are like the mule, and when offspring are mated with one another they are infertile. These scientists believe that this result indicates enough genetic difference to establish those named as separate species, even though when mated back to one parent species some of them were fertile in a limited way.

Experiments of this kind are of great value, particularly when the species or subspecies have separate ranges, and hence no chance to meet in nature. As valuable as such information is, it is well to keep in mind, when one is interested in the general biology of butterflies, that it is equally valuable to study and chart the ways of either subspecies or species, since both are parts of the on-going evolutionary process.

5

THE TIGER SWALLOWTAILS
AND OTHERS

Within this family the Tiger Swallowtails are North America's particular glory of color and presence. In other parts of the world, members are often simply black and white, or black with greens and blues in contrast, and there are very colorful species, but nowhere else appears the dazzling brightness of this yellow which expresses the light of the sun against the black borders of night. The Tiger Swallowtails are also abundant, unafraid, even familiar, being as much at home in a cultivated flower garden as along streams and rivers. In summer they will lazily fly back and forth between shrubs such as the purple butterfly bush and the pink abelia, or such brilliant herbs as crimson zinnias and scarlet geraniums, tying the garden colors together with their movements.

Members of the Tiger group have no Old World relative, and seem to be of temperate North American origin. Here they were affected in much the same way as the American species of the Old World Swallowtail group by the succession of Pleistocene ice ages. Of six species, one now occupies the eastern U.S., while a nearly identical second species prevails in western mountains and valleys. In the mountains along the eastern side of Mexico there is a third species, also nearly identical, which retreated farther southeasterly. In the western U.S. flies a fourth pale replica of these, as well as the (fifth) Two-tailed species which also flies in most of Mexico. From the Texas border to Honduras and

El Salvador flies the sixth species, with three tails. The last may not belong to the group, despite its similar pattern, as the early stages differ and it extends into the tropics on the southern end of its range.

All members of the Tiger Swallowtail group are distinguished by a large black "V" which occupies the inner half of the hind wing, and five (or in one case four) vertical black bars on the forewing, the innermost two of which extend the tops of the V. (Some Kite Swts. have a similar pattern, but their ground color is white rather than yellow, and their tails are long and slender.)

TIGER SWALLOWTAIL GROUP

12.   *Papilio glaucus*   L. 1764

EASTERN TIGER SWALLOWTAIL   Pl. IV, Figs. 1,2,5,7,8.

Expanse: avg. 80-140 mm   **Tails:** 12-15 mm
Description. The ♂ and one form of the ♀ are yellow; a second form of ♀ is dark. In this species the UnFW has separate submarginal spots. [In *P. rutulus* (13) these form a band]. There are exceptions to this rule in Nebraska.

UnHW: The second. third, and fourth submarginal spots are orange, as is the first. (In *P. rutulus* all of these spots are usually yellow, but the first may be streaked with orange; hence the next three are more diagnostic.) There are exceptions, notably in spring broods of se. Canada and ne. U.S., in which the orange of *P. glaucus* is reduced or absent.

Dark form of female. UpFW brownish black with only a narrow line of clouded submarg. spots. The old pattern of black bands shows through faintly. UpHW dark, with prominent round orange spot at upper end of submarg. row; others dull white. Submarg. band of blue spots prominent. UnW lighter and vertical bars more visible.

Note: This form mimics the Pipevine Swt. (58), as does the Spicebush Swt. (18). The latter also has a round orange spot on forward edge of HW, but set well in toward body.
Habitat. Woodland—particularly deciduous woodland where it frequents the edges—along roads and paths, streams and rivers. Adapts readily to orchards and gardens. Along roadsides the adults feed

on clover, thistles, Joe-Pye Weed, bee balm, and milkweed, but they also feed on puddles in barnyards in which they find nitrogen and sodium. In gardens the species is notably attracted to lilacs and butterfly bush.

Flight. In Florida and s. Georgia, common from Mar. to Nov.; 3 broods. From Atlanta north, first brood in April. In Penn., 3 broods: May-June, mid-July, mid-Aug.-Sept. In Illinois, 2 broods: April, and early Sept.

Food Plants. Larval food plants are more diverse for this species than for any other Swt. Said to feed on plants of 13 families, of which Rosaceae, Oleaceae, Salicaceae, Corylaceae and Magnoliaceae are most important. They have special favorites in particular areas, e.g., willow in New England. Some of the important food plants are:

tulip tree, *Liriodendron*	cottonwood, *Populus*
wild cherry, *Prunus*	ash, *Fraxinus*
birch, *Betula*	willow, *Salix*
cucumber tree, *Magnolia*	basswood, *Tilia*
mountain ash, *Sorbus*	

Early Stages. Mature larva smooth green; on third segment of thorax there is an orange eye spot with a black pupil. In the Eastern Tiger the "eyes" are formed of a single spot. In the three western species the spot is made of a double element.

Distribution.

Alaska.

Canada from e. coast to B.C., where it splits range with next species.

Eastern U.S., overlapping with *P. rutulus* (13) in the Dakotas and Neb.

Wash.: A few records in Okanogan Highlands; may represent the introgression of characters, rather than Eastern Tiger species.

Wyo.: Subsp. *canadensis* reported in Weston Co., which is adjacent to Black Hills of S.D.

Colo.: Eastern border of state; valleys of South Platte and Arkansas Rivers.

Neb.: Eastern half.

Kansas: Becomes rare in w. part of state.

Texas: s. and c. parts of state.

Note. Dark ♀ form absent from Canada (a rare record or two) and n. U.S., scarce in Florida. In Bibb Co., Ga., 95% of ♀♀ dark. In Ill., yellow ♀♀ uncommon. In Penn., summer ♀♀ are 35% dark on Coastal plain, 20% in Bucks Co. Dark form rare in Allegany State Park, N.Y.

Subspecies.

12.a. *P. glaucus glaucus* L.

As described above.

12.b. *P. glaucus canadensis* Roths. & Jordan 1906

Pl. IV, Fig. 2.

A small, Canadian Life Zone subsp., found in Alaska, Canada, n. New England, e. New York, n. Mich., Minn., Wis., and perhaps n. N.D.; reported from Weston Co., Wyo.

There is also a small-sized spring from of *g. glaucus.* In Wis. *g. canadensis* is found only in the north and is single-brooded; it can be distinguished by its having UnFW submarg. spots in band form, and by the black outer margin of hind wing which is much narrower than in spring form of *g. glaucus.*

Shapiro (1974) refers to a vernal f. "canadensis" which is limited to the e. part of New York state; it is the only *glaucus* found in the Adirondacks, but it is evidently sympatric with the larger kinds found elsewhere in e. N.Y. The relationship of spring f. "canadensis" to subspecies *canadensis* deserves further study; it is possible that sibling species are involved.

12.c. *P. glaucus australis* Maynard 1891

Very large in size and ochreous in color. Occurs in Florida and s. Georgia along with *g. glaucus* and probably should be listed as a late-season form, rather than a subspecies.

13. *Papilio rutulus* Lucas 1852

WESTERN TIGER SWALLOWTAIL   Pl. IV, Figs. 3,4.

Expanse: 70-100 mm   **Tails:** 12-15 mm
Description. Sexes similar. Resembles eastern counterpart (12) and was long regarded as a subspecies, but genetic and biological studies have established its independent status. Differences given under *P. glaucus* (12).   78

Habitat. Nearly unrestricted as to altitude and life zones, except Arctic-Alpine. Equally at home in city parkways, high mountain forests, or sagebrush of basin and mesa country, but usually prefers water courses where its larval food plants grow. Above 10,000 ft it becomes rarer and single-brooded.

Flight. As early as Feb. in s. Calif., April farther N, May in Wash. state, June and July in high mountains; through Sept. in most of range.

Food Plants. Basically willows (*Salix*), cottonwoods and aspen (*Populus*). On Sycamore (*Platanus racemosa*) in s. Calif. below 4000 ft, and on European green alder (*Alnus*). Also reported on ash (*Fraxinus*) at Davis, Calif.

Early Stages. Mature larva bright green; yellow false eye-spots on thorax with blue "pupil", bordered in black. In earlier stages larva has tubercles with bristles on all abdominal segments. (In *P. glaucus* these bristles are on only last three segments.) Larva may change from green to red just before pupation.

Distribution. Canada: B.C. U.S.: Wash., E to Badlands of N. Dakota where rare, S, possibly along w. border of Neb. Found throughout Colo. In New Mexico at least as far E as Capulin Nat. Mon., 30 mi. E of Raton. Baja Calif.: Reported from Meling Ranch and Santa Cruz, both in n. part of Baja. All western areas lie within these boundaries.

Forms and Possible Subspecies. Form "ammoni" Behrens 1887. According to original descr.: "A very peculiar form, in which the ground color of all the wings is a deep but rather dull orange color." Markings of upper surface said to be broader; the specimen came from Nev., presumably near Reno.

13.a. *P. rutulus rutulus* Lucas

As described above.

13.b. *P. rutulus arizonensis* Edwards 1883

Said to come only from higher mts. of s. Ariz.: the Chiricahuas, Catalinas, and Santa Ritas. Its black markings are more emphatic. This variety is said to occur in the Pine Valley Mts. of Washington Co., Utah (Tidwell & Callaghan, 1972). If true, this must be a form, rather than a subsp.

13.c.   *P. rutulus arcticus*   Skinner 1906

This subsp. is another interesting possibility which should be examined and settled. The types came from Eagle, Alaska, and the Athabasca River in Alberta, Can. According to F. Martin Brown this small version of *rutulus* differs from *P. glaucus canadensis* in the same way as the species, i.e., UnHW submarg. spots in *canadensis* show at least some orange; *arcticus*: all submarg. spots are yellow. It is single-brooded, while typical *rutulus* has 2 or 3 broods. Brown states that the *rutulus* from the Canadian Rockies and out onto the plains along the rivers tends to be *arcticus*.

14.   *Papilio alexiares*   Hopffer 1866

MEXICAN TIGER SWALLOWTAIL   Pl. V, Fig. 6.

Expanse: 78 mm (one specimen)   **Tails:** 6 mm
Description. Apparently this Swt. is more closely related to its Western counterpart (13) than to the Eastern Tiger Swt. (12). (Brower 1959.) In shape it is intermediate between *P. glaucus* (12) and *P. rutulus* (13). Salient distinction: UnHW has three burnt-orange marks, in the form of long triangles, between discal cell and marginal black band.
Habitat. Lower mountains of e. Mexico, where there are damp ravines and also open fields; 500 m (1600 ft) alt. On the n. and s. ends of its range it flies together with the Two-tailed and Three-tailed Swallowtails.
Flight. April through June, at least.
Food Plants. Unknown.
Early Stages. Unknown.
Distribution and Subspecies.

14.a.   *P. alexiares alexiares*   Hopf.

UpFW: Yellow portions shaded with black scales; outer marginal black band wider than yellow median band. UnHW orange triangles smaller than in next subspecies. Range: Mts. of Veracruz: Cuesta de Misantla.

14.b.   *P. a. garcia* Roths. & Jordan 1906

Black bands of both wings narrower; UnFW yellow submarg. bands interrupted at veins. Range: Mts. of Nuevo Leon and Coahuila; Monterrey, N.L.; Hacienda Vista Hermosa, Villa Santiago, N.L., at 500 m (1600 ft) alt.

15.   *Papilio eurymedon* Lucas 1852

PALE SWALLOWTAIL   Pl. V, Fig. 1.

Expanse: 75-95 mm   **Tails:** 11-14 mm

Description. Sexes similar. Same basic pattern as rest of group, but ground color pale yellow to almost white, and all black markings broader, sometimes leaving little white area. UpFW, submarg. row of lineal spots, row often fading out toward rear. In collections could remotely be confused with Zebra Swt. (37); in nature they have distant ranges. The Zebra Swallowtail has a long slender tail; the Pale Swt. has a broader, spatulate tail which is proportionally shorter.

Habitat. Less fond of water courses than its relatives, and will fly on dry hill or mountain sides. Low elevations in coastal hills, and even ocean bluffs. Does not enter dry valleys. In the Sierra Nevada of Calif. it ranges from 2000 to 10,000 ft. In Wyo. it is a widespread species in Transition and Canadian Life Zones— 7500 to 10,000 ft.

Flight. S. Calif.: March into Aug. Ore. and Wash.: May through July. Wyo. and Utah: June-July.

Food Plants. Over most of its range, limited to family Rhamnaceae: coffee berry (*Rhamnus californica*); red-berry (*R. crocea*), both of these called buckthorn. On various species of wild-lilac, (*Ceanothus*). In Colo. it is *C. fendleri*. In s. Calif. it is reported on *Prunus ilicifolia* (a wild plum) and also on domestic prunes, both of family Rosaceae.

Early Stages. Mature larva soft green with yellow-and-black false eye. These eye-spots are narrower than in *P. rutulus* (13) or *P. multicaudata* (16).

Distribution. British Columbia, and down Coast Range hills and mountains of entire west coast to n. Baja Calif. Santa Cruz Isl., off Santa Barbara, Calif. Wash.: Entire state.

Ore.: Records lacking for some coast cos., and absent in arid regions along n. border E of Cascades; absent from Malheur Co.

Calif.: Coast ranges to s. end of state; Sierra Nevada; absent from interior valleys and deserts.

Idaho, Wyo., w. Colo.: above 6000 ft.

Utah: Apparently scarce; mts. of Cache, Rich and Weber Cos., 5500 to 8000 ft, Wasatch Mts., west drainage.

New Mexico: No records, but might occur in nw. mts.

Forms. The f. "albanus" Felder and Felder 1864, is of smaller size, clearer white, with submarg. spots nearer margin. From Wash.

16. *Papilio multicaudatus* Kirby 1884

TWO-TAILED TIGER SWALLOWTAIL   Pl. IV, Fig. 6.

Expanse: 85-130+ mm   **Main Tails:** 12-24 mm

Description. Sexes similar. Same pattern as in rest of group, but the UpFW black stripes are narrower than on Western Tiger Swt. (13), with which this species often flies. Prime distinction is the extra tail, set in toward body, of half (or less) the length of the main tail. There is also a tooth at the anal angle but it is never as developed as in the Three-tailed Swt.

Habitat. Tolerates hotter and drier situations than other species of group, but is still attracted to moist canyons, even in desert mts. More restricted to lower altitudes than the Pale Swt. and Western Tiger Swt. Hoffmann (1940b) refers to its Mexican habitats as "temperate and cold regions up to 2800 meters."

Flight. June through Aug. in Calif., but some May flights. June and July in Rocky Mts., but in Colo. there may be an uncommon spring flight in April, comprising small individuals. Feb. to Nov. in s. Texas. Through Oct. in Morelos, Mex.

Food Plants. Choke cherry (*Prunus virginiana*) over much of range, incl. Mexico; western choke cherry (*P. v. demissa*) in n. Calif.; wild plum (*P. americana*) in Colo.; service berry (*Amelanchier* spp.) in B.C.; all in family Rosaceae. Various ash (*Fraxinus*), dwarf ash (*F. anomala*) in s. Calif; privet (*Ligustrum vulgare*)in Texas; these in family Oleaceae. Hop tree (*Ptelea trifoliata* var. *angustifolia*) in Texas, family Rutaceae.

Early Stages. Mature larva soft green; false eye-spots with prominent dark outlines; round spots on abdomen with light centers. In late summer, many larvae change from green to red, just before pupation.

Distribution.

Canada: E. B.C. and w. Alberta.

Wash.: E of Cascades in Arid Transition and Upper Sonoran Life Zones.

Ore.: All counties E of Cascades; one coastal record, Coos Co.

Calif.: Can reach coast, but largely confined to hot, inner Coast Range. Abundant in Mt. Shasta and Lassen areas; river woodlands of Central Valley and foothills of Sierra Nevada, S to Greenhorn Mts.; Tehachapi Mts.; in s. Calif., most records are well inland, except one at Anaheim; n. slope of San Gabriel Mts., and Gilroy Canyon in Providence Mts. of e. Mojave Desert.

Nev.: Toiyabe Range in cent. Nev.; probably many other ranges.

Mont. and Wyo.: Generally distributed in mts.

Colo.: Throughout below 8000 ft.

New Mex.: In all mts.

Ariz.: Common in Chiricahua, Santa Rita and other mts. of the se. quadrant.

Utah: Statewide in mts. to 9000 ft.

Texas: Edwards Plateau W to El Paso and N through Panhandle; San Antonio and Bexar Co.

Kans.: Stray in Scott Co., w. part of state.

Neb.: Common W, and flies in all w. half.

N.D.: Common in Badlands; flies in w. half.

Mexico: Length of country from e. slopes of Sierra Madre Oriental to the western ranges. Specific locations: Santiago, Nuevo Leon, 500 m (1600 ft); Tancitaro, Michoacan, 2000 m (6600 ft). It is the only sp. of Tiger Swt. which flies in Mexico City. Specimens from Morelos and Michoacan are very large and ochreous yellow.

Note. The larger individuals of this magnificent butterfly are unmatched for the showers of light they spread with each rapid wingbeat. While they are very swift in flight they may also turn and drift in circles as effortlessly as a hawk.

17. *Papilio pilumnus* Boisduval 1836

THREE-TAILED SWALLOWTAIL   Pl. V, Fig. 2.

Expanse: 80-95 mm   **Main Tails:** 18-20 mm

Description. Sexes similar. Differs from the Two-tailed Swt. (16) by having the tooth at anal angle of HW developed into a third tail nearly as long as the second. The main tail is linear and narrow, with a yellow border down inner margin and around tip. (In the Two-tailed Swt. (16), the main tail is curved, and the yellow border stops midway.)

> UpFW: Black bands much broader than in Two-tailed Swt.
> UpHW: A broad rusty-orange area at base of black "V".
> UnFW: Outer margin brownish black and broad. (In Two-tailed, outer margin is a narrow black line.)

Habitat. Hoffmann (1940b) says it inhabits temperate and tropical regions; perhaps not the humid tropics. In El Salvador it is recorded from shady woods, above 2100 meters (7000 ft). The lower Rio Grande in Texas.

Flight. There are records from Jan. (Tepic) to Sept. (Victoria).

Food Plants. "Laurel".

Early Stages. Larva green, with eye spots, but head is brown. Before pupation, the back becomes pale brown, and then pink.

Distribution. All of Mexico to Guatemala, where it is common. Occasional records from Honduras and El Salvador. There was a 19th century record for Ariz., published in Wheeler Report. In Los Angeles Co. Museum is a specimen from Falcon Res., Tex., from Zapata or Star Co. Specific Mexican records: Monterrey, Santiago, Linares, and Galena, all in Nuevo Leon; Ciudad Victoria, Tamaulipas; Orizaba and Las Vegas, Veracruz; Jalapa, Tabasco; Ochuc, Chiapas; state of Guerrero at 800 meters (2700 ft); Tepic, Nayarit.

Note. Although this species resembles the preceding ones in pattern, it may be transitional between the Tiger Swallowtails and the next group, since in its early stages it is more like the latter.

THE SPICEBUSH SWALLOWTAIL GROUP

This small group comprises only two species, the adults of which look nothing like the Tiger Swallowtails just described; but the larvae are, again, smooth, green, humpbacked, and with eye spots on the last segment of the thorax. Resemblance between larvae is thought to be a more reliable guide to relationships than are wing patterns. One need only think of the mimics which have completely changed their adult patterns to resemble those of models—or the Zebra Swallowtail (37) whose adult resembles the Tigers in pattern but belongs to a different genus—in order to see why early stages are a more reliable guide to relationships.

18. *Papilio troilus* L. 1758

SPICEBUSH SWALLOWTAIL   Pl. V, Figs. 3,4.

Expanse: 80-115 mm   **Tails:** 9-12 mm

Description. Sexes similar except for HW colors. This species, particularly in its undersides, mimics the inedible Pipevine Swallowtail (58), but it need not fool the human observer.

UpFW: Black, with submarg. row of ovate creamy spots and fringe spots to match; sometimes a faint partial row of median spots.

UpHW: Prominent round orange-red spot on forward edge of wing; this spot is usually greenish white in summer ♂♂ (but not in spring ♂♂); base of wing black; outer part greenish in ♂ and bluish in ♀; submarg. spots lunulate and clouded with blue.

UnHW: Has submarg. row of orange spots, as does the Pipevine Swt.; but this species also has a curving median row of orange spots by which it can be identified. There is a blue wash between these rows which imitates the more metallic blue-green lustre of the Pipevine Swt.

Habitat. Borders of shady woods seem to be a first choice, but it also inhabits open fields and gardens. In N.Y. it lives in the oak-hickory association; in Wis. it prefers deep deciduous forests; but in New Jersey it is common in pine barrens. In all areas the adults are partial to honeysuckle, clover and thistle blooms.

Flight. As early as end of Jan. in s. Georgia, but there and in Florida mainly from Mar. to Nov. In s. Wis.: June-July. In Allegany State Park, N.Y., first brood in June-July, second in latter part of Aug. Kansas: April-Oct.; same in D.C.

Food Plants. Sweet bay (*Magnolia virginiana*); spicebush (*Lindera benzoin*); red bay (*Persea borbonia*); sassafras (*Sassafras albidum*). First of these belongs to Magnolia fam., others to Laurel fam. Prickly ash (*Zanthoxylum americanum*) of Rue family.

Early Stages. Mature larva dark green above and lighter below. Eye spots on 3rd seg. of thorax are light yellow, with a double "pupil". On first seg. of abdomen there is a pair of buff spots with black borders, about half the size of the eye spots.

Distribution. Southern Canada as far W as Manitoba. All of eastern U.S., but rare in n. N.Y. and New England. Western borders are: common in s. Ill., but becomes rare in nw. cos.; rare in s. quarter of Wis.; one record from Minn.; single record from N.D., and one from Omaha, Neb.; common in e. Kansas, becoming rare to the W; three records for Colo; common in e. Texas, breeds as far W as Kerr Co.; not found in s. Texas.

Subspecies.

18.a.   *P. troilus troilus* L.

As described above.

18.b.   *P. troilus ilioneus* Smith 1797

Submarginal spots on both wings larger, and those on HW with less blue, often pale yellow. Blue sometimes extends down tail. This subsp. is found in Florida, in coastal Georgia, and it is the Texas representative.

19.   *Papilio palamedes* Drury 1770

PALAMEDES SWALLOWTAIL   Pl. V, Fig. 5.

Expanse: 80-140 mm   **Tails:** 10-12 mm

Description. Sexes similar. Black with light-yellow fringe, and submarg. spots which are ovate on FW and broadly lunate on HW. Median band of light-yellow spots which are irregular in shape; spots of band are offset outward on FW and fused into a solid band on UpHW. Spot at anal angle is black, with blue half circle above and a rufous mark beneath, or sometimes both above and below.

The unique mark on this species is a thin yellow line on UnHW, running parallel to abdomen along entire wing, and usually continued faintly on UnFW.

Being median banded, this species has a remote resemblance to the Giant Swt. (20) and members of that group. In *palamedes* the band of HW passes through just the tip of discal cell, or misses it (in the Giant Swt. band passes across base of cell, or includes all of cell in band).

Habitat. A coastal-region species, and when farther inland likes areas with standing water. Fred Nauman reports that in Georgia the adults are particularly fond of the light blue flowers of pickerel weed (*Pontederia cordata*) which grows all summer in standing water or boggy spots. The adults also roost together in the red bay trees.

Flight. Occasional in late Feb. in much of its range, and some fly as late as Nov.; most, April to Aug. in Texas; Mar. to Dec. in Florida; Mar. to Nov. in Georgia.

Food Plants. Red bay (*Persea borbonia*) and sassafras (*Sassafras albidum*) of Laurel family. Sweet bay (*Magnolia virginiana*) of Magnolia fam. has been listed, but apparently the species is limited to the Laurel fam. and will accept avocado and *Nectandra* spp. under lab. conditions.

Early Stages. Mature larva a pale velvety green with lighter flecks. False eye spots are black, with glossy black "pupil" in a circle of orange. This species is said to winter over in either larval or pupal stage. All of preceding species hibernate in pupal stage only.

Distribution. Resident from Dismal Swamp, Va., southward, but may also be found on coastal plain of Maryland and near Cape May, N.J. Strays have been taken in Wilmington, Delaware, and even on Staten Isl., N.Y. All of Florida. In Georgia, common in coastal area, becoming less common inland, and rare in the Piedmont. It follows the Gulf states to Texas where it flies in e. part and Coastal Bend. Strays have been taken in Kerrville and Ft. Worth. It is uncommon in Miss. Valley as far N as Missouri.

Note. While this species is in its own way as handsome as the Tiger Swallowtails, it resembles them not at all and only the similarity of the caterpillars proves a close kinship.

Subspecies.

19.a. *P. palamedes palamedes* Drury

As described above.

19.b. *P. palamedes leontis* Roths. & Jordan 1906

This Mexican version has small median-band spots on UpFW;

in ♀, smaller than submarg. spots. Diagnostic point is lack of yellow bar in apex of UpFW cell. UnHW median band narrow, orange, and the blue spots outside this band are larger. Yellow bar of UnHW reduced to a line.

Distribution. NE. Mexico; Monterrey, Nuevo Leon; Vista Hermosa, Villa Santiago, N.L., 500 m (1600 ft); 35 km W of Linares, N.L. Author has specimens from Madera, Chihuahua, on the e. slope of the Sierra Madre Occidental far to the W of previous records (Aug. 1969).

ADDITIONAL SPECIES

Papilio esperanza   Beutelspacher, 1975.
(*Revista de la Sociedad Mexicana de Lepidopterologia*, Vol. I, No. 1, p. 3)

ESPERANZA SWALLOWTAIL

Expanse. 85 mm (FW length 51-2 mm)

Description. Black bases and outer margins on both wings, between which there is a broad, yellow median band, including a yellow bar in upper end of discal cell. This is a member of the *glaucus* group but lacks the black stripes and V of the other tiger swts. It is the most distinctively different new swallowtail species in our time.

Habitat. Sierra de Juarez, Oaxaca, Mexico. At 1700 m (5600 ft) alt.

Flight. March, for the two known specimens.

6

GIANTS AND ARISTOCRATS

We come to yet another group of yellow-banded swallowtails, the Thoas group, but these often display their yellow in a festoon, 'draped' from the tip of one fore wing down through the middle to the body and back up to the other tip, much as bunting is draped on festive occasions. The ground color is a rich brown or intense black, and in size the various species trend from large to very large. On the undersides of the more familiar species the black areas are heavily washed with light yellow, so as these butterflies sail lazily overhead the appearance is that of a large yellow butterfly with a few dark zig-zags and dark narrow wing margins.

While the first three groups of Swallowtails, the Old World, Tiger and Spicebush belonged to temperate North America, the locus of the Thoas group is shifted southward and the affinities of its species are circum-Caribbean. They may have originated in that area, but even if not, their development took place in the region. While four of the thirteen species of this group are restricted to the islands of the West Indies, seven other species are found in the area covered by this book. It is a curious fact that even though Mexico, Central America and the West Indies are their real home, all but one of these species at least touch on the southern fringes of the United States, in Texas and Florida. Only one species, the Giant Swallowtail, is firmly a resident of the U.S., and it also flies as far south as Costa Rica. The account begins with this species (20) because it is familiar; but it is thought to be a recently separated species, while the Bahaman Swallowtail (26) represents the progenitor of the group.

THOAS GROUP

20.   *Papilio cresphontes*   Cramer 1777

GIANT SWALLOWTAIL   Pl. VI, Fig. 1. (See 20.b)

Expanse: 85-140 mm   **Tails:** 12-18 mm

Description. Sexes similar. Ground color dark brown. UpFW: anterior spots of yellow median band separate, 3rd from top long, 4th short; submarg. row is combined with median spots on upper half of FW, so only 3 or 4 lower spots appear, and upper submarg. spot is close to band, not to margin. UpHW: Yellow band solid and placed near base of wing; submarg. spots are broad lunules set well in from margin. Abdomen yellow, with dark stripe along back, none underneath.

This and next species (*P. thoas*) are often nearly identical in appearance. Many distinctions have been suggested: the Giant Swt. usually has three submarg. spots on FW while *P. thoas* often has four. None of these distinctions is certain, and the only way to tell is to examine the tip of the abdomen. In ♂♂ of *cresphontes* there is an open space between the claspers, when viewed from above. In *P. thoas* there is no such space.

Habitat. Likes the bright sunshine of open places, clearings in deciduous forests in U.S., or cultivated fields, gardens and citrus groves in Mexico and Central America. Likes roadsides where flowers grow, and also forest edges where flowers bloom. Seems to be local in occurrence.

Flight. In s. part of range it flies the year around. In Florida it is infrequent in Jan.-Feb. In Texas., absent Dec.-Jan. In Delaware Valley, has two broods: May-June and Aug.-Sept.; in Neb., the same; Kansas: May-Oct.; Wis.: late May through mid-Aug.

Food Plants. Prickly-ash (*Zanthoxylum americanum*); hercules club (*Z. clavaherculis*); wild lime (*Z. fagara*); hop tree (*Ptelea trifoliata*); gas plant (*Dictamnus albus*); rue (*Ruta graveolens*); lemon and orange trees (*Citrus* spp.); "matasano" (*Casimiroa edulis*). All are in the Rue family. Also Laurel, Willow and Pepper families.

Early Stages. Mature larva is the "orange dog", brown with a buff saddle on fore part of abdomen, a similar patch over end of abdomen. A buff band around top of head and sides of thorax.

Distribution.

Canada: Rare or strays in S; London, Ont., and nearby.

U.S.: Common in Florida; becomes scattered northward as far as Mass.; rare in Mich. and Minn.; sporadic in all of Illinois; s. 1/3rd of Wis. only; sparse records in se. quarter of Neb.; Kans.: uncommon and local resident; e. Colo.: a few records of strays; found in at least 32 Texas cos. The species is commonest in central and southern states.

Until recently the above list would have served for the U.S., but quite recently the species has extended its range. In 1961 it was observed in the Imperial Valley of se. Calif. It has become common about the town of Brawley where adults feed at lantana blossoms. In 1971 two larvae were found on citrus trees in Fresno Co. of c. Calif., so it is apparently following citrus groves up that state. One surmise on how it came to Calif. is that the species spread on native larval food plants from mts. of n. Mexico to mts. of s. Ariz. and thence to the citrus groves of the Salt River Valley and Yuma Mesa. It is common in Phoenix, Ariz. where the larval food plant is ornamental sour orange. It is not a great leap across the desert to the s. Calif. orange groves.

Mexico: entire country including Baja Calif., where it has been taken at La Paz and San Pedro.

Subspecies and Forms.

20.a. *P. cresphontes cresphontes* Cram.

As described above.

20.b. *P. cresphontes pennsylvanicus* Cherm. & Cherm. 1945

This is the subspecies illustrated in Plate VI, Fig. 1. Spots of UnFW larger, more elongated, yellow on UnHW more extensive. Similar specimens are said to have been taken in Florida, in which case this would be a form rather than a subspecies. Form: "melanurus" Hoffmann (1940a) from Guerrero, Mex. has all-black tails. A dark form is also noted in Florida.

21. *Papilio thoas autocles* Roths. & Jordan 1906

THOAS SWALLOWTAIL Pl. VI, Fig. 2.

Expanse: 80-100 mm **Tails:** 12-14 mm

Description. Sexes similar. The figure illustrated is not typical, in that it has the extra spot within FW cell and is of a bright yellow. These are characteristics of the subsp. *nealces* of Nicaragua, but similar specimens from Mexico are mentioned by Brown (1943) and Serrano (1972), the latter assuming that the two subsp. are not distinct.

Usually the yellow of *thoas autocles* is paler than that of *P. cresphontes* (20). A good but not perfect distinction is on UnFW: *thoas* has broad submarg. yellow spots which almost join median band, leaving only a thin dark line between on upper wing. (In *P. cresphontes* the submarg. spots do not extend inward that far.) The best distinction is that there is no gap between claspers in *thoas*; if the thumb nail is rubbed across them there will be no click.

While this species and the last look alike, the genitalia differ and the chromosome counts of the two species also differ, which is unusual among Swallowtail species.

Habitat. Very fond of feeding at flowers, and even more adjusted to cultivated fields, gardens and towns than *P. cresphontes*. Hoffmann (1940b) lists it as inhabiting all of *temperate* Mexico, but it is also found in some tropical areas in Veracruz and S.L.P. In El Salvador it flies everywhere, from sea level to 1800 m (6000 ft).

Flight. Year around in many places, with 5 to 7 broods a year.

Food Plants. Cultivated *Citrus* in Mexico; in Tuxtla Mts. on *Piper marginatum* (candle bush) and *P. kerberi*. Also on Laurel family.

Early Stages. Mature larva with dark olive green head, body a dirty white variegated with yellow; some olive on back. In general it resembles a bird-dropping. Life history in Comstock and Vazquez (1960), and Ross (1964b).

Distribution. U.S. records, such as Kansas and Colo., probably originate in either mistakes or windblown strays. Does occur along lower Rio Grande River in s. Texas. Common from Texas border to Ciudad Victoria. Occurs throughout much of Mexico and south to Nicaragua where it merges with *P. thoas nealces*.

Note. *Papilio thoas thoas* flies in Brazil and the Guianas.

22.   *Papilio ornython* Boisduval 1836

KING ORNYTHION SWALLOWTAIL   Pl. VII, Fig. 5♀, Fig. 6♂

Expanse: 85-95 mm   **Tails:** 8-10 mm

Description. Sexes usually differ. Male: Pattern similar to those of *P. cresphontes* (20) and *P. thoas* (21). Differs in having row of submarg. spots of UpFW parallel to margin and near edge; the spots are thin and linear; also differs by having tails short, broad and without the spatulate shape and yellow spot of preceding two species. ♂ differs from *P. astyalus* (23) in the narrower median band, and lack of a yellow spot in apex of discal cell.

Female: A few are like ♂, or may differ from ♂ by having upperside nearly all brown, by having only vestigial pattern, or by having the ♂ pattern but in dull color. Some resemble *P. astyalus* ♀, but shape of tail differs.

Habitat. Both temperate and tropical areas. Favors citrus groves.

Flight. Records known to author run from April through December.

Food Plants. Citrus.

Early Stages. Mature larva like that of *P. thoas*, but smaller, more yellow.

Distribution.

U.S.: McAllen and Mission, Hidalgo County, Texas, to Brownsville, Texas.

E. Mexico: Monterrey, Nuevo Leon; Galena, N.L., at 2000 m (6600 ft); Ciudad Victoria, Tamaulipas; ♂♂ common in May on road from Mante, Tam., to Valles and on to Tamazunchale, San Luis Potosi; Yucatan.

Mesa Central. W. Mexico: Along valley of Rio Balsas, Michoacan, and N through Jalisco; probably farther. Baja California Sur: (San Antonio vicinity).

23.　　*Papilio astyalus pallas*　Gray 1852　　　Pl. VI, Figs. 5,6.

PALLAS SWALLOWTAIL　　　　　　(formerly *P. lycophron pallas)*

Expanse: 90-110 mm　　　　　　**Tails:** ♂: 9-11 mm ♀: 3 mm

Description. Sexes unlike. Male differs from *P. ornythion* (22) by having broader median band and a spot in anterior end of cell of FW—often a double spot—and from the next sp., *P. androgeus* (24), by having thick submarg. spots on HW, and narrower median bands.

Female: Black, with a few buff or yellow spots beyond apex of FW cell; submarg. spots of FW near margin. UpHW with three rows of spots: submarg. row yellow, middle row blue, inner row either red, or blue with a terminal red spot, as in Pl. VI, 6. Tail very short, or just a tooth.

93

Habitat. Males fly in open sunshine, but ♀♀ confine themselves to the woods and are thereby rarer in collections. From sea level to 700 m (2300 ft).

Flight. Records known to author run May through September.

Food Plants. Citrus: orange and lime.

Early Stages. Like others of this group.

Distribution.

U.S.: McAllen to Brownsville, Texas.

E. Mexico: Victoria, Tamaulipas; El Bañito, San Luis Potosi; Rio Blanco, Veracruz.

Central Mex.: Mesa de San Diego, Puebla; n. Chiapas.; Tuxtepec, Oaxaca.

W. Mexico: Apatzingan, Michoacan; Culiacan, Sinaloa.

Subspecies. This subspecies, *a. pallas*, reaches Costa Rica, but it is not found in Honduras or El Salvador. Three other subsp. extend the range to Argentina.

24. *Papilio androgeus epidaurus* Godman & Salvin 1890

ANDROGEUS SWALLOWTAIL Pl. VII, Figs. 1,2,4.

Expanse: 105-115 mm **Tails:** ♂: 13-15 mm; ♀ as ♂, or short (5-6 mm).

Description. Sexes differ. Males are the brightest members of the Thoas group, with yellow median band taking up more than half the area of HW. ♂ differs from *P. astyalus pallas* ♂ (23) by lack of large yellow submarg. spots on UpHW; instead these are reduced to faint, linear lunules. Foremost spot of submarg. row ovate and bright yellow. Tails long and narrow (in *a. pallas* they are broader and shorter.)

Females: Roths. and Jordan (1906) state that there is only one form of the ♀, but it seems to be variable. UpFW with yellow patch at anterior end of discal cell varying from almost invisible to large (if place data are correct), as in Pl. VII, Fig. 2. The latter resembles some South American forms in this respect. UpHW with a broad expanse of iridescent blue-green which includes much of the cell. Two rows of submarg. lunules, which are blue or yellowish. Tails variable, as on plate.

Habitat. Males on flowers in open fields, taking water from puddles in sand, flying along lakeshores, or well above forest canopy, and everywhere reported fond of hilltopping. ♀♀ seldom seen in open.

Flight. Records known to author run from May through August.

Food Plants. *Zanthoxylum elephantiasis* in Tuxtla Mts. of Veracruz. Mandarin orange (*Citrus reticulata*) in El Salvador. Any citrus.

Early Stages. Mature larva: head tan, body dark gray to black with many white streaks and blotches. All segments with slight knobs which have crescent-shaped blue marks at base. Osmeterium orange. Life history in Ross (1964a).

Distribution.

Does not reach U.S.

Mexico: s. Tamaulipas southward to Yucatan. Chiapas (Hoffmann reports it in Soconusco District). N along west coast through Jalisco (Puerto Vallarta) to Sinaloa and its borders with Durango.

Subspecies. *P. a. epidaurus* is found also in Cuba and Haiti, and from Mexico to Panama. There are two other subsp. in South America.

The next two species of the Thoas group approach the United States from Cuba and the Bahamas, touching southern Florida. They are not found in Mexico.

25.   *Papilio aristodemus ponceanus* Schaus 1911

SCHAUS'S SWALLOWTAIL   Pl. VI, Fig. 3.

Expanse: 85-95+ mm   **Tails:** 12-14 mm

Description. Sexes similar. Differentiated from *P. thoas* (21) and *P. cresphontes* (20) by the UpFW submarg. spots' being parallel to margin of wing; from *P. astyalus* (23) and *P. androgeus* (24) by its very narrow median band, which maintains nearly the same width across both wings. Differs from *P. ornythion* (22) by having a long tail with yellow border. *P. aristodemus ponceanus* has a single tail, dark centered and yellow margined. The next species, *P. andraemon bonhotei*, has two tails, centered with yellow, at least toward tips.

The signal mark of this subspecies is a broad, rusty patch on UnHW at outer end of discal cell and around sides of cell for a short way. This patch is missing from Cuban specimens, of another subspecies.

Habitat. *P. a. ponceanus* prefers the shady areas within hardwood hammocks; *P. cresphontes* (20) flies in same area but keeps to the sunnier, open spaces.

95

Flight. April into June.

Food Plants. Larva feeds on sea amyris (*Amyris elemifera*) or wild lime (*Zanthoxylum fagara*), both of Rue family.

Early Stages. Mature larva: maroon background with cream-yellow blotches along sides and around ends; prolegs white; light blue spots on back. Described and illustrated in Rutkowski (1971).

Distribution. Formerly as far inland as Brickell hammock near Miami; now on keys: Key Largo; Lower Matecumbe Key; several remote keys NE of Key Largo. Islands of Biscayne National Monument, Florida.

Subspecies. In addition to this U.S. subsp. there is one on Cuba, and the nominate subsp. is Haitian.

26.   *Papilio andraemon bonhotei* Sharpe 1900

BAHAMAN SWALLOWTAIL   Pl. VII, Fig. 3.

Expanse: 75-80 mm   **Tails:** Main 13-16 mm, Inner 4-7 mm

Description. Sexes similar, dark brown, with a nearly straight, solid, median band of yellow. Distinguished from other members of group by having two tails, one long and yellow with dark borders, the other short and pointed. This species has a prominent yellow cross bar in anterior end of FW discal cell.

Habitat. Flies in the dense hammocks, and on the trails which transect that vegetation. It also flies over open water from one island to another, even in normal weather, and seems able to utilize hurricanes for transportation, which is quite an adaptation.

Flight. Emerges in April and May, and only tattered specimens are found at the end of May.

Food Plants. Key lime (*Citrus aurantifolia*), sour orange (*Citrus aurantium*); also other citrus, and garden rue (*Ruta graveolens*) in part of its range.

Early Stages. Mature larva: head dark brown, thorax ashy gray and reddish brown; two white lines along side, with two blue spots above; abdomen olive brown, with white patches on sides; osmeterium white; white saddle on 8th and 9th segments.

Distribution. For a long time it was thought to be wind-blown strays which were seen in Florida (record for Long Key in Oct. 1955). But a survey of the islands in Biscayne Nat. Monument, off e. coast of Dade Co., Florida, in 1972, showed that this and the preceding species were abundant, as many as 100 being seen in a day. Quite possibly this species will spread to the mainland.

Subspecies. In addition to this race in Florida and the Bahamas, there are races in Cuba and on Grand Cayman Isl.

Note. This species is thought to be the original from which the other two lines in the Thoas group descended. In the same view *P. aristodemus* (25) forms a link between *P. thoas* (21) and *P. cresphontes* (20) on the one hand, and *P. astyalus* (23) and *P. androgeus* (24) on the other. *P. andraemon* is vigorous and a current colonizer, having invaded Jamaica as recently as 1945, where it is thriving, possibly at the expense of resident species.

7

SOME HOWS AND WHYS OF
LARVAL FOOD PLANTS

A reader who has followed the lists of larval food plants given with each species will perhaps have a mixed impression at this point. On the one hand the plants seem to present a random sampling from a number of families and genera, but on the other hand it is hard to miss the fact that some groups of Swallowtails have a narrow range of choices, as witness those of the Thoas group which concentrate on citrus and other members of the Rue family, or the Old World Swallowtail group whose members feed on plants of the Parsley family, with excursions into sagebrush and citrus. The Tiger Swallowtails, in contrast, are most diverse in food plant choices, feeding on trees and shrubs belonging to a number of families.

In answering some of the "whys" of these selections the first thing to note is that butterflies lack the kinds of choices humans have for balancing their diets. In a simple sense there is no choice, because the female lays her eggs on only a certain kind of plant, or one of only a few kinds. Hence, the newly hatched caterpillar usually has no alternative to feeding on that plant or dying, as it often does if there has been a mistake. The broader truth is that the caterpillar is restricted because its kind has become adapted in a physiological sense to that particular plant. Any given plant species is nutritionally unbalanced, and once the physiology of an insect species has adapted to this limited fare it is totally committed, unless the species finds other plants with similar qualities.

A caterpillar is adapted not only to the limited food type offered by the host plant but it is adapted as well to all of the secondary plant substances, ranging from familiar essential oils to recondite chemical compounds, some of which are toxic. It is obvious that such complex adaptations cannot be a matter of choice of the moment by either the egg-laying female or the newly hatched caterpillar. They are, of course, determined in the long evolution of the butterfly family through its species, as well as in the correlative evolution of a number of plant families. Plant species react to attack, and it seems probable that some of the poisonous plant substances were selectively developed because of the protection they afforded from most herbivores. However, once Swallowtails had mastered these toxins they had little competition for plants that were inedible to most other creatures—and some of the butterflies themselves thereby became inedible.

If we think in terms of butterflies and plants together, a correlation stands out: butterflies and flowering plants (Angiosperms) originated at about the same time, and most authorities today incline to the belief that the first family of true butterflies was the Swallowtails. Among the first orders of flowering plants is a group historically referred to as the Woody Ranales, and in more modern classifications as the order Magnoliales. In that group are the Magnolia family, the Laurel family, and the less familiar Annona family—to which pawpaw and custard apple belong. In the same subclass with Magnoliales, and probably derived from it, is the order Aristolochiales which contains only a single family, Aristolochiaceae, familiar to us in the dutchman's pipe vine, Virginia snakeroot, and other native species. The major development of these plant families is in the tropics, where the greatest elaboration of the Swallowtail Family also took place.

Several families of these first, primitive orders of flowering plants seem to provide the majority of the basic larval *food* plants for the various genera of the Swallowtail Family; but two other plant families which provide species important as larval foods, the Parsley and Rue families, are not in the least primitive. That poses the question of why some members of the Swallowtail Family later deviated from the original choice of food plants. One answer is related to the present distribution of these plant families. The Rue family, to which citrus plants belong, is universal in its distribution, being found in *both* tropical and temperate regions, while the Parsley family is characteristic of temperate and even cold regions. On the wild parsleys members of the Old World Swallowtail group are able to thrive in Alaska and on high mountains in the West.

Thus, there is *advantage* to be gained in shifting to these families of plants in that they enable the colonizing of vast *non*tropical areas, and species of the genus Papilio have often accepted the opportunity. There are, of course, members of the Laurel family in North America, but it is essentially a tropical and subtropical family. The Magnolia family has a most interestingly discontinuous distribution. It is centered in the tropics of Southeast Asia and Indonesia, an area which is thought to be the original home of the Swallowtail Family; but the Magnolia family has a second center of distribution which extends northward from Panama and includes the southern part of the U.S. Except for a few strays, it is not found elsewhere. The other important food-plant family, the Annonaceae, is tropical and the Kite Swallowtails, which are specialized toward it, are largely tropical butterflies.

One can see the advantage of using the newer food plants as stepping stones into new areas; but that poses the question of how it was *possible* to shift—what did the old and the new food plants have in common? If you crush the leaves of sweet bay or sassafras and then crush the leaves of prickly ash or citrus, or the leaves of any member of the Parsley family, your nose will tell you that they all have one thing in common: aromatic substances. In form, the oil glands of these virtually unrelated plants are identical, and all of them contain essential oils of one kind or another.

These essential oils are made up of "isolates", which are divers chemical compounds that contribute aromatic qualities. Citral is an aldehyde which provides the characteristic lemon and orange odors of that group of plants; the odors and tastes of camphor and rue are contributed by ketones, and a still different compound is responsible for the bitter principle in rue and others. It is remarkable that oil of sassafras from the primitive Laurel family contains the same odor and substance as oil of fennel from the advanced Parsley family. Following the thought another step, it will be recalled that the Oregon and Baird's Swallowtails have shifted from the Parsleys to the sagebrushes of the family Compositae. Specifically, the shift is to green sage, *Artemisia dracunculus*, of circumboreal distribution, which grows not only in the arid regions of the West, but also in gardens, where it has the domestic name of tarragon.

Tarragon is the well known flavoring herb, and it contains, as do anise and fennel, the compound, anisic aldehyde, which gives the characteristic odor and flavor to all three plants.

In addition to essential oils there are other secondary plant substances which are relevant, and of these the most important are called alkaloids. These are hard to define, but they are chemical compounds with more or less toxic properties. Morphine is an alkaloid from the poppy, while the substance extracted as curare from species of *Strychnos*, and used as poison on arrow heads, contains another. Nicotine and caffein are likewise alkaloids, as is quinine. Alkaloids are found in a limited number of plant families, several of which are important in providing food plants to the Swallowtails. Plants of the families Aristolochiaceae, Magnoliaceae and Annonaceae contain the alkaloids magnoflorine and berberine. In the Laurel family are found berberine and menisperine. Rue family species of the genus Zanthoxylum also contain this same set of alkaloids. Presumably the butterfly species which has adapted to these toxic compounds in one plant family will have some ability for coping with them in other plant families. However, the limits of choice are narrow, and there is an instance of one U.S. species which can thrive on certain species of Aristolochia, but will die if the egg is laid on *a different species* of the same genus.

By leaving out widely divergent food plants one can make a considerably simplified table of Swallowtail groups and their larval foods.

Papilio (Old World Swallowtail Group):
Parsley family, with offshoots to green sage (Sunflower family) and to the Rue family.

Papilio (Tiger Swallowtails and Allies):
E. Tiger on Magnolia and Willow families, plus many others, esp. Ash and Rose fams. Three-tailed Swt. on Laurel fam. Two-tailed on Rue fam., but also on Ash and Rose fams. W. Tiger on Willow fam. Pale Swt. on Rhamnus. Spicebush Swt. on Magnolia, Laurel and Rue fams. Palamedes Swt. on Laurel family.

Papilio (Thoas and Anchisiades Groups):
Rue family.

Eurytides (Kite Swallowtails):
Primarily on Annonaceae, but also on Laurel and Magnolia families.

Parides and **Battus** (Cattle Hearts and Gold Rims):
Primarily genus *Aristolochia*, but also Rue family and Black Pepper family (Piperaceae).

Subfamily **Parnassiinae** (Parnassians)
In general, *Aristolochia*, but our *Parnassius* on Saxifragaceae, Crassulaceae, or Fumariaceae, some of the latter containing alkaloids similar to those of poppy.

Subfamily **Baroniinae** (*Baronia*, Short-horned Swallowtail):
The single very primitive species feeds on *Acacia cymbispina*. There is an important "why" to be studied here. Another Mexican acacia, *A. farnesiana*, produces oil of cassie which contains anisic aldehyde, the compound mentioned earlier, but chemical analyses of *A. cymbispina* are not yet available.

The neatness of the above list has tempted students to draw conclusions on the development of the Swallowtail Family, based on food plants. One of these theories, developed before the food plant of Baronia was known, holds that aristolochia feeders were primary. They may have been, but much depends on which genera of True Swallowtails are determined to be the oldest on other grounds. It is equally possible to assume that the Aristolochia Swts. form one branch of the True Swallowtails, culminating in the genus *Parides*, while the second branch may have begun with ancient species of *Papilio* that fed on Magnoliales, then evolved toward the Kites, which are more specialized in both food plants and wing structure. While that is not the way most scholars now see the matter, it is evident that further study of food plants and their distribution will be important in constructing a Swallowtail family history.

PLATE IX

1. Torquatus Swallowtail, *Papilio torquatus tolus* ♂ (32). Yucatan, Mexico. July 1961.

2. *Papilio torquatus tolus* ♀ (32). Oaxaca, Mexico. July 1972.

3. Victorinus Swallowtail, *Papilio victorinus victorinus* ♂ (33). Dos Amates, Veracruz, Mexico. November 1969.

4. Morelius Swallowtail, *Papilio victorinus morelius* ♂ (33). Acapulco, Guerrero, Mexico. January 1962.

5. Black Giant Swallowtail, *Papilio garamas* ♂ (35). Morelos, Mexico. 14 June 1966.

6. Electryon Swallowtail, *Papilio abderas electryon* ♂ (36). Oaxaca, Mexico, at 1500 m (5000 ft). March 1973.

PLATE X

1. **Zebra Swallowtail,** *Eurytides marcellus* ♂, f. "marcellus" (37). Linglestown, Penn. 28 April 1974. Early spring form.

2. *Eurytides marcellus* ♂, f. "telamonides" (37). Linglestown, Penn. 20 June 1974. Late spring f.: longer tails.

3. *Eurytides marcellus* ♂, f. "lecontei" (37). Lewis and Clark State Park, York Co., Penn. 10 August 1956. Summer f.: tail bordered white; red of anal eye spot small.

4: *Eurytides marcellus* ♀, f. "floridensis" (37). Winter Gardens, Florida. June 1959.

5. **Dark Zebra Swallowtail,** *Eurytides philolaus* ♂ (38). Ciudad Victoria, Tamaulipas, Mexico. 20 May 1971.

6. *Eurytides philolaus* ♀ f. "niger" (38). Ciudad Victoria, Tam., Mexico. 21 May 1971. Most ♀♀ of this species are like ♂♂.

PLATE IX

1

2

3

4

5

6

106

PLATE X

1

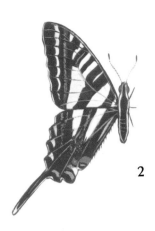

2

3

4

5

6

PLATE XI

(Mimics among Kites; see Plate XIV for Models)

1. The Thymbraeus Mimic, *Eurytides thymbraeus* ♂ (43). Morelos, Mexico. August 1959.

2. *Eurytides thymbraeus aconophos* ♂ (43). Malinalis, s. Mexico. September 1946.

3. The Belesis Mimic, *Eurytides belesis* ♂ (42). San Quintin, Chiapas, Mexico. 15 June 1970.

4. The Phaon Mimic, *Eurytides phaon* ♂, f. "phaon" (44). Mapastepec, Chiapas, Mexico. 5 August 1963.

5.a. *Eurytides phaon* ♂, f. "eridamas" (44). Santiago, Tuxtla Veracruz, Mexico. 12 August 1973.
  b. *E. phaon* ♂, 2nd variant f. UpHW for comparison. (44)

6. The Branchus Mimic, *Eurytides branchus* ♂ (41). Presidio, Mexico. June 1969.

PLATE XII

1. Oberthuer's Zebra Swallowtail, *Eurytides oberthueri* ♂ (39). Figure drawn after photograph of type specimen in Roths. & Jordan (1906). Specimen examined had light areas pale greenish-white. Yaxchilán, Chiapas, Mexico, at 150 m (500 ft). June 1974.

2.a. Lesser White Page, *Eurytides agesilaus neosilaus* ♂ (45). Yucatan, Mexico. October 1960. This eastern subspecies intergrades with that figured in 3.
  b. Under surface of same specimen.

3. *Eurytides agesilaus fortis* ♂ (45). Salada, Colima, Mexico. 4 July 1958. The western subspecies.

4. Epidaus Swallowtail, *Eurytides epidaus epidaus* ♂ (40). Veracruz, Veracruz, Mexico. 20 July 1972.

5. Northern White Page, *Eurytides protesilaus penthesilaus* ♂ (46). San Quintin, Chiapas, Mexico. 27 May 1970.

6.a. *Eurytides epidaus fenochionis* ♂ (40). Salada, Colima, Mexico. 18 May 1968. See text for size.
  b. Under surface of same specimen.

PLATE XI

1

2

3

4

a

5

b

6

PLATE XII

1

2
a

b

3

4

5

6
a

b

PLATE XIII

1. Marchand's Kite Swallowtail, *Eurytides marchandi* ♂ (47). San Quintin, Chiapas, Mexico. 16 June 1970.

2. Calliste Kite Swallowtail, *Eurytides calliste* ♂ (49). Chiltepec, Oaxaca, Mexico. 11 February 1971.

3. Indians' Kite Swallowtail, *Eurytides lacandones* ♂ (48). San Quintin, Chiapas, Mexico. 22 August 1972.

4. Salvin's Kite Swallowtail, *Eurytides salvini* ♂ (50). Chiapas, Mexico. May 1961.

5. Alopius Cattle Heart, *Parides alopius* ♂ (52). Morelos, Mexico. September 1971.

6. Zestos Cattle Heart, *Parides sesostris zestos* ♂ (54). Dos Amates, Veracruz, Mexico. 11 October 1971.

PLATE XIV

1.a. **Red and Blue Cattle Heart,** *Parides photinus* ♂ (51). Yucatan, Mexico. July 1961. Note open scent fold.
  b. Under surface of same specimen.

2. **Montezuma Cattle Heart,** *Parides montezuma* ♀ (53). Tampico, Tamaulipas, Mexico. 27 September 1974.

3. **Polyzelus Cattle Heart,** *Parides polyzelus* ♂ (55). Pichucalco, Chiapas, Mexico. 20 July 1973.

4. **Mylotes Cattle Heart,** *Parides arcas mylotes* ♂ (57). Pichucalco, Chiapas, Mexico. 18 August 1973.

5. **Iphidamas Cattle Heart,** *Parides iphidamas* ♂ (56). Tapachula, Chiapas, Mexico. 21 August 1960.

6. *Parides iphidamas* ♀ (56). Tapachula, Chiapas, Mexico. 21 August 1960.

PLATE XIII

1

2

3

4

5

6

114

PLATE XIV

1

a   b

2   3   4

5   6

PLATE XV

1.a. **Pipevine Swallowtail,** *Battus philenor* ♀ (58). Brevard, North Carolina, at 3000 ft. July 1970. Orange spot is near anterior edge of UnHW; in some specimens it may show through on UpHW, especially in transmitted light.

b. *Battus philenor* ♂ (upper surface), f. "acauda". Acapulco, Mexico, at sea level. January 1962.

2.a. **Polydamas Gold Rim,** *Battus polydamas* ♂ (59). Miami, Florida. 7 September 1969.

b. UnHW.

3.a. **Godman's Gold Rim,** *Battus eracon* ♂ (60). Drawing after plate in Godman & Salvin, *Biologia Centrali-Americana: Insecta: Lepidoptera–Rhopalocera.* Specimens examined: ♂ & ♀ from Comala, Colima, Mexico at 600 m (2000 ft). September 1973. See text for UpHW spots.

b. UnHW.

4.a. **Belus Varus Gold Rim,** *Battus belus varus* ♂ (61). Oaxaca, Mexico. July 1972.

b. UnHW has diagnostic row of white dots between margin and red submarginal bars (lacking in *B. laodamas*, Fig. 5b).

5.a. **Laodamas Gold Rim,** *Battus laodamas copanae* ♂ (62). Oaxaca, Mexico. July 1972.

b. UnHW.

6.a. **Lycidas Gold Rim,** *Battus lycidas* ♂ (63). Chiapas, Mexico. July 1955.

b. UnHW.

PLATE XVI

1. Alaskan Parnassian, *Parnassius eversmanni thor* ♂ (64). Eagle Summit, Alaska. 30 June 1973. Coll.: Marc Grinnell.

2. *Parnassius eversmanni thor* ♀ (64). Same data as ♂.

3. Phoebus Parnassian, *Parnassius phoebus* ♂ (66). Big Horn Co., Wyo., 9000 ft. 2 August 1963.

4. *Parnassius phoebus* ♀ (66). Big Horn Co., Wyo., 10,000 ft. 2 September 1967.

5. Clodius Parnassian, *Parnassius clodius* ♂ (65). Branscomb, Mendocino Co., Calif. 14 June 1974. Coll.: Marc Grinnell.

6. *Parnassius clodius* ♀ (65). Same data as ♂.

7. Short-horned Swallowtail, *Baronia brevicornis* ♀ (67). Morelos, Mexico. July 1971.

8.a. *Baronia brevicornis* ♂ (67). Guerrero, Mexico. August 1958.

   b. Underside of same ♂.

PLATE XV

PLATE XVI

8

APPEARING INEDIBLE OR FIERCE

In this chapter the last three groups of North American *Papilio*, the Anchisiades, Torquatus and Homerus groups, are described, and it will be seen that their face to the world is very unlike that of the bright-winged species which have gone before, as these latter species are predominantly dull brownish black. The reason for this shift to new and somber mein is that all of the Anchisiades group, and the females of the Torquatus group, are mimics of the red-banded black Aristolochia Swallowtails, which are inedible and hence serve as models for the unprotected. The Homerus group reminds one that black is itself a warning coloration in butterflies, suggesting to predators that the meat under the dark exterior may be anything but tasty. These butterflies are large, with heavy veins in the wings, and the anterior margins of the forewings are serrated, which contributes to their formidable aspect.

ANCHISIADES SWALLOWTAIL GROUP

Of the thirteen member species in this group one has a lengthy distribution, from the southern tip of Texas to Argentina, while half of the others are South American. Of the remaining six, four are Mexican and Central American, while two are limited to Caribbean islands. All species are mimics of the Cattle Heart Swallowtails of the genus *Parides*

121

and probably also of the Gold Rims of the genus *Battus*; but this mimicry has not progressed as far as minute imitation, and some species simply show black wings with red spots on the hind wings and thorax, which gives only a very crude approximation of the models. Other species are developing a white patch on the forewings that is characteristic of certain *Parides* females, but this mark shows up in some individuals and not in others. The Anchisiades group has another striking difference from other *Papilios* in that its caterpillars are gregarious; when resting, or after a night of feeding, they gather together at the bases of limbs or tree trunks to sleep.

There is some difficulty for the observer or collector in that these Anchisiades Swallowtails are often seen flying with their models; furthermore, there is a group among the Kite Swallowtails which also mimics these same models, making three sets of similar butterflies. It so happens that the red pigment of this Anchisiades group of mimics is different from that of the models, appearing as a rather dull rose rather than the bright red of *Parides*; also, the black ground color is a *dull* black, lacking the iridescent blue sheen of some *Parides* models.

The Anchisiades group of genus *Papilio* is characterized by *dull* red pigments in the spots and dots on the hind wing. *Apparent* hue ranges from a grayed brick red to a grayed crimson, depending on the angle of illumination and the angle of view (see Plate VIII). This variation is caused by a slight iridescence arising in diffraction of light by the lamellate (layered) fine structure of all of the scales of the wing, which act as 'gratings' and contribute a varying amount of spectral blue to the color of the spots. The result might be called a dull rose. Marginal spots may be a dull orange, as in *P. pharnaces* (28).

If one is in Mexico and faced with an unknown black swallowtail with red spots, the three sorts, belonging to three different genera, can be separated as follows:

Genus **Parides** (models).
These have red spots on head, thorax, and base of abdomen, with at least some red spots on middle abdominal segments. Toward the tip of the abdomen there is a line of red running down one side, under, and up the other side.

Genus **Papilio** (mimics, Anchisiades group).
Lighter red spots on head and thorax, and a spot on upper side of first abdominal segment only. No red marks toward tip of abdomen.

Genus **Eurytides** (mimics, Kite Mimic group).
No red spots or lines on abdomen (*E. phaon* excepted), except sometimes at base of first segment. Instead there are several red spots on base of hind wing, and also a red line running down inner margin of HW. Together these serve to imitate abdominal red spots on models.

If, on the basis of these rather simple distinctions, the butterfly proves to be a *Papilio* of the Anchisiades group, there will be five choices open, and of these only the first two are common.

27.   *Papilio anchisiades idaeus* Fabr. 1793

IDAEUS SWALLOWTAIL   Pl. VIII, Figs. 1,2.

Expanse: 85-95 mm   **Tails:** None
Description. Base of UpFW black; outer half a lighter arc giving a sunrise effect. A white patch extends through anterior end of FW cell in ♀, and sometimes in ♂. Wing margin a thin white line, often worn off.

UpHW black, with white fringe spots and a slight projection at end of each vein. Two rose-red dots (sometimes confluent) at anal angle, followed by three rose-red bars, often with some white in them.

UnHW with two rows of spots, outer pinkish white, inner incomplete, consisting of five rose or rust spots. UnFW may or may not have white streaks around apex of cell.
Habitat. Well domesticated and prefers cultivated citrus groves, hedgerows and flower gardens. Has potential as a pest, but in at least two areas seems to be controlled by a parasitic wasp.
Flight. Records known to author run from April to November.
Food Plants. Native FP, *Casimiroa edulis*, white sapote, a tree of the Rue family, which grows to 2000 m (6600 ft) in e. Mexico. Also any cultivated citrus.
Early Stages. Mature larva has brown head and tiny tubercles, body greenish brown with streaks, lines and flecks of white or cream. Prolegs brown or yellowish. Osmeterium yellow. There are two rows of short, fleshy tubercles along back. Life history described in Ross (1964a).
Distribution. This subspecies from se. Texas to Panama. All of e. Mexico.   Chiapas (San Quintin); Fortin, Veracruz; Victoria, Tamaulipas; Arroyo del Calabezas, San Luis Potosi.

Subspecies. There are two other races in South America.

28. *Papilio pharnaces* Doubleday 1846   Pl. VIII, Fig. 4.

PHARNACES SWALLOWTAIL   (Name refers to a buckwheat plant which has clusters of round, rosy flowers.)

Expanse: 85-95 mm   **Tails:** sometimes none; if present 6-7 mm

Description. UpFW like *P. anchisiades idaeus* (27), except no white patch. The HW has two rows of rosy spots; inner row incomplete at anterior end. On HW of both sexes the anterior fringe spots are white, the posterior red and white.

A rather poor mimic of *Parides photinus* (51), with which it flies; *P. photinus* has a narrow tail, bright scarlet spots, and a blue iridescence to its black.

Habitat. Flies along margins of woods in either temperate or tropical areas.

Flight. Records available to author run April through October.

Food Plants. Citrus and other members of Rue family.

Early Stages. Unknown.

Distribution. Mexico only. Along Pacific side: Comitan, Chiapas; Oaxaca; Guerrero; Valley of Rio Balsas; Michoacan, Jalisco and Sinaloa. In c. Mexico: Cuernavaca, Morelos; La Piedad, Michoacan; Leon, Guanajuato; Querétaro, Qro.; Jacala de Ledesma, Hidalgo. The latter is the northeasternmost record.

Forms. The f. "dissimilis" Vazquez, from Chiapas, has white streaks on UnFW; f. "paucimaculata" has reduced number of spots on UpHW.

29. *Papilio erostratus* Westwood 1847   Pl. VIII, Figs. 5,6.

CUPID'S QUILT SWALLOWTAIL   (A literal trans. of the Latin)

Expanse: 85 mm   **Tails:** 7-10 mm

Description. Sexes differ. Male: UpHW with a single row of creamy, lunulate submarg. spots. Female: Two rows of rosy spots on both surfaces of HW, plus rosy but white-edged spots along margin. Similar to *pharnaces* (28) but spots of two main rows are larger. Best distinction from *pharnaces*: tails long and slender, rather than broad and tapering.

Habitat. Tropical rain forest and other natural jungle in e. part of range. In El Salvador, flies between 600 and 2000 m (2000 and 6600 ft).

Flight. Records known to author run from April to September.

Food Plants. Wild plants of the Rue family. (?)

Early Stages. Unrecorded.

Distribution. Yucatan Pen.; interior of Chiapas (Comitan, Tapachula, at 800 m, 2700 ft). Cuautla, Morelos; Acahuizotla, Guerrero.

Note. Females of this species are good mimics of *Parides photinus.*

30. *Papilio erostratinus* Vazquez 1947

VAZQUEZ SWALLOWTAIL Pl. VIII, Figs. 7,8.

Expanse: 58-82 mm **Tails:** 6-9 mm

Description. A smaller edition with smaller spots than *P. erostratus* (29). UnHW of ♂ has the inner row of spots rosy red, outer row white (in *erostratus* both rows are rosy red). The rosy spots of inner row, UpHW of ♀, are quite small, and on underside these are widely bordered with a color blacker than rest of wing. This might be a northern subspecies of *erostratus* (?).

Habitat. Type came from a citrus grove in a temperate valley surrounded by mountains with pine-oak woodland.

Flight. April to Nov.; two broods: April-May, and Oct.-Nov.

Food Plants. Leaves of orange trees, and other citrus.

Early Stages. According to Dr. Escalante (in corresp.) the larva is similar to larva of *P. multicaudatus* (16), but smaller; the body is greenish with black and mulberry-colored (*moradas*) spots.

Distribution. E. Mexico: Sierra Madre Oriental: Jalapa, Veracruz at 1500 m (5000 ft); San Luis Potosi; Nuevo Leon; Tamaulipas. SC. Mexico: near Nexaca, Puebla.

31. *Papilio rogeri* Boisduval 1836

ROGER'S SWALLOWTAIL Pl. VIII, Fig. 3.

Expanse: 80-95 mm **Tails:** None

Description. Sexes differ. Both sexes have black base to FW with lighter outer arcs. Both have UpHW fringe spots large at forward edge, and diminishing. UnFW has arc of creamy white streaks. Male: UpHW with three coral-red dots posterior to end of cell; on under surface these are continued with a black line to forward edge of wing. Female: UpHW may have two complete rows of coral-red spots, or only partial rows. HW more rounded than in ♂.

Habitat. Natural, tropical evergreen forest.

Flight. Records known to author happen to be August and September.

Food Plants and Early Stages. Unrecorded.

Distribution. Mexico: Pisté, near Valladolid, Yucatan; Quintana Roo. British Honduras.

TORQUATUS GROUP

There are seven species in this predominantly South American group, and the species for which it is named has a Mexican representative, *P. torquatus tolus*, which is one of six subspecies. The sexes of this species differ greatly, as the male is yellow-banded while the female is a generalized mimic.

32. *Papilio torquatus tolus* Godman & Salvin 1890

TORQUATUS SWALLOWTAIL   Pl. IX, Figs. 1,2.

Expanse: 75-85 mm   **Tails:** ♂ 12-15 mm; ♀ 7-8 mm

Description. Sexes unlike. Male: black with yellow median band (narrower in Mexican *tolus* than in other subsp.) that is terminated half way to apex of FW. Above this is a narrow cross bar. HW with row of straw-yellow submarginal spots and fringe spots; two red spots at anal angle, anterior one longitudinal, posterior one transverse. Female: UpFW black and with or without white patches at anterior end of cell. UpHW with three or four coral-red bars and two dots of same color at inner margin and at anterior end of row. Tails of ♀ short and narrow, of ♂ long and spatulate.

Habitat. Females stay within forested tracts of both temperate and subtropical areas, while males venture into open.

Flight. July to October; primarily July-August in e. Mexico.

Early Stages. These larvae are not gregarious; eggs are deposited singly. In color and pattern mature caterpillars are like those of *P. thoas* (21) (information from Brazilian ssp.). There are prominent tubercles in rows along back of mature larva.

Food Plants. Lemon and tangerine, in Brazilian subspecies.
Distribution. E. Mexico: Tabasco; Veracruz; Tuxtepec, Oaxaca; as far
N as Cd. Victoria, Tamaulipas, but rare in all of east. W. Mexico:
Guerrero; Colima; Nayarit; Jalisco.

HOMERUS GROUP

The magnificently beautiful swallowtails of the Homerus group
are as unlike the common vision of a butterfly—a delicate creature bearing intricately designed and colored patterns on its wings—as can be
imagined. These, instead, are stark in design, dark in base color, coarse-
ly veined, particularly on the forewings, and they are powerful flyers,
preferring the buoyant air to resting places. The famous Jamaican
species for which the group is named is the largest member of genus
Papilio, and its mainland relatives are of ample size. While the Anchisiades and Torquatus groups in this chapter and the Thoas group of
Chapter VI are closely related, as shown by their early stages, the
Homerus group is well separated from these and appears here only because these species stand last in the order of American Papilios. The ten
or eleven species of the group are rather evenly distributed, from Mexico
to southern Peru and northern Argentina. As presently seen there are
either three, or four, species inhabiting Mexico, depending on the status
given to *P. abderus* (36). *Papilio diazi* (34) is the most recent addition
to the North American Swallowtail fauna.

33. *Papilio victorinus* Doubleday 1844

VICTORINUS SWALLOWTAIL Pl. IX, Fig. 3.

Expanse: 95-110 mm **Tails:** none
Description. One of the two ♀ forms differs from the ♂. Male: Brownish black base with row of yellow submarg. spots on both wings,
spots of HW crescent shaped. FW with inner row of similar spots
which is incomplete on upper surface, but complete on under surface and curving to forward edge of wing at a point just beyond
cell. UpHW with inner row of yellow spots, separated from submarg. row by a few buffy-blue patches. Female: One form like
♂ but with larger spots on UpHW inner row. Second form, "am-
phissus", has broad green or bluish band in place of the inner row
of spots on HW.

Habitat. The immediate vicinity of woods; in sunny glades of seasonal forest and along roads in montane rain forest of Tuxtla Mts., Ver. In El Salvador it flies at elevations of 600 to 1200 m (2000 to 4000 ft).

Flight. Records from January to November.

Food Plants. Species in family Lauraceae.

Early Stages. Mature larva has pale gray head; second segment gray with a pale-green transverse band; fourth segment with a few black spots; and a transverse band between fifth and sixth segments. *P. v. morelius* larva described in Comstock & Vazquez (1960).

Distribution. Temperate and tropical regions of e. Mexico as far N as Nuevo Leon and Tamaulipas. It is interesting that this subspecies follows the e. coast into Honduras, but in El Salvador it is found only in the c. and w. parts of that country.

Subspecies.

33.a. *P. victorinus victorinus*

As described above.

33.b. *P. victorinus morelius* Roths. & Jordan 1906

Pl. IX, Fig. 4.

Differs from *v. victorinus* by smaller size (90-95 mm). Inner row of spots on UpFW dim or obsolete; those on HW reduced to dots, and there is a continuous row of bluish spots between these and submarg. row of yellow lunules.

A chrysalis of this race was found on an avocado tree (Laurel fam.), though it could have arrived there from some other plant.

Distribution. Comitan, Chiapas; Oaxaca; s. Puebla; Morelos; Valley of Rio Balsas, Guerrero; s. Michoacan; at least sparingly in Jalisco.

34. *Papilio diazi* Racheli & Sbordoni 1975 (See Bibliography)

DIAZ SWALLOWTAIL Pl. VI, Fig. 4.

Expanse: 103 mm (in one ♂) **Tails:** 8 mm; inner tooth 3 mm

Note. Dr. Racheli generously forwarded a copy of his description of this new species, but as the book was already set in type before that was received the description below is based upon a single specimen of the insect, a color photograph supplied by A. Diaz

Frances, and relevant excerpts gleaned from Dr. Racheli's description.

Description. *P. diazi* differs from *P. victorinus* in having a tail and a tooth. (Genitalia of the two species differ considerably; illustrated in description.) Base of the median band of FW is set well in from the submarg. spots, and it angles at once toward the anterior end of the cell, turns at that point, and faint spots (not indicated on fig.) parallel the cross vein of the cell to the forward edge of the wing. (In *P. v. morelius* the FW median band is usually absent; in *P. v. v.* it consists of three or four spots from base, close to and parallel with submarg. spots.)

UnFW median band nearly solid, not made up of spots. (Band very broad in holotype, but not in author's specimen.) UnHW median-band spots are multicolored (in both subsp. of *victorinus* these are round red spots, each completely margined with black). In *P. diazi* these spots comprise a light-yellow, crescentic inside margin, holding a half circle of rusty red; the red is based with a black stripe and is rounded toward outside with a patch of blue scales. This series of bright spots is set against the red submarg. lunules which are common to both species. (The colorful median band of UnHW was present in the holotype, as the orange is said to be "dusted with yellow proximally." In the paratype this band was entirely of orange spots, as in *P. victorinus morelius*.)

Habitat. Restricted to a small area in Morelos where it flies with *P. victorinus morelius*.

Flight. Author's specimen taken in Nov., holotype taken in Dec., and paratype taken in May.

Food Plant and Early Stages. Unknown.

Distribution. Tepoztlan; the single ♂ from Yautepec, both in Morelos, Mex.

35.　*Papilio garamas* (Hubner) 1834

BLACK GIANT SWALLOWTAIL　　　　　　　Pl. IX, Fig. 5.

Expanse: 100-120 mm　　　　**Tails:** main 13-16 mm, inner 6-7 mm

Description. Sexes sometimes differ. Black, with narrow yellow band in form of an arc of a circle—in spread specimens most of circle is evident. Smaller yellow arc toward apex of FW. HW has submarg. lunules which are yellow above and orange below. Row of blue spots between yellow band and submarg. row.

129

Females: two forms, one being much like ♂, the other without yellow band, on upper side at least. Both inner row of UpHW lunules and submarg. row are bright rufous; these separated by complete row of blue patches. A very large and striking, predominantly black butterfly set off with a HW necklace of bright blue.

Habitat. Forests, to 2000 m (6600 ft), at least.

Flight. March to November.

Food Plants. Avocado.

Distribution. Central and w. Mexico: Jalisco; Michoacan; Valley of Rio Balsas; Guanajuato; Mexico, D.F.; Puebla; Tepoztlan and Cuernavaca, Morelos; Oaxaca and interior of Chiapas. If next species is joined (see note under 36.) the e. Mexican range of *garamas* is from Nuevo Leon through Veracruz.

Forms. The ♀ f. "amisa" (dark form as described above). The f. "baroni"; described as a subsp. by Rothschild and Jordan (1906), but reduced by Hoffmann; underside paler; from Guerrero.

36. *Papilio abderus electryon* Bates 1864

ELECTRYON SWALLOWTAIL   Pl. IX, Fig. 6.

Expanse: 90-95 mm   **Tails:** main, 8 mm, not spatulate; sub., 4 mm

Description. Like preceding species, but smaller, and tail narrow; UpHW without submarg. spots; yellow band narrows at forward margin; UnHW, the orange streaks at veins on outer edge of band extend nearly to submarginal orange lunules.

Habitat. Shady woods. In El Salvador it flies above 2000 m (6600 ft) altitude.

Food Plants and Early Stages. Unknown.

Distribution. E. Chiapas; mts. of Oaxaca at 1500 m (5000 ft). W. El Salvador.

Note. *P. abderus* has a dark ♀ f. "amerias". Hoffmann makes *abderus* a full species (and some Mexican scholars today agree), the e. Mexican equivalent of *P. garamas* (35). Hoffmann lists *electryon* as a subspecies from e. Chiapas. *P. abderus*, whether species or subspecies, differs from *P. garamas* by having no submarg. spots on UpHW, and the yellow median band of HW usually enters the discal cell. If *abderus* is not a valid species, *electryon* is instead *garamas electryon*, as it is listed by Serrano and Serrano (1972). The question obviously needs study.

As the account of the genus *Papilio* closes here, it is worth noting that 36 species have been listed for North America, while all of South America has only 31 species in this genus. Perhaps a half dozen of the North American species will be dropped after further study, but others may be added and we have not counted the Caribbean species with affinities to mainland North America. The result, then, is one of parity in number of species between the North and South American divisions of the genus, and although the genus may have had a tropical origin it seems to have adapted well to northern and temperate climates in the New World.

THE KITE SWALLOWTAILS

Genus **Eurytides** Hübner 1821

Formerly both Old World and New World Kite (or Kite-tailed) Swallowtails were grouped in the single genus, *Graphium*. As there are slight structural differences in the New World members, these were separated and placed in the genus *Eurytides*, which comprises 51 American species, as opposed to 82 species in the Old World genus. Most of the latter inhabit either the African or the Indo-Australian region. However, the two genera are not far apart and a number of species have look-alikes in the opposite genus. The American genus has been divided into five groups, and all of these groups are represented in the area covered by this book.

9

ZEBRAS, MIMICS, WHITE-PAGES, AND BRIGHT COLORS

As the title for this chapter suggests, the Kite Swallowtails are a very diverse group, a fact which excites interest but also requires a little close study to fix their diversities clearly in mind. Despite this diversity, many species do have hind wings of triangular shape ending in very long, slim tails, which configuration makes their popular names of 'Kite', 'Kite-tailed', or even 'Swordtail', appropriate. A number of species display patterns of black stripes on white or off-white ground color, which makes the 'Zebra' name, given to the U.S. representative, fitting as well.

The Kites, of the genus *Eurytides*, sometimes show two characters which were never present in the genus *Papilio*. One of these is a tendency for the light colored portions of the forewings to be more or less transparent. A second difference is that many of the males in this genus have a modified edge along the inner abdominal margin of the hind wing. The Fluted Swallowtails were so called because that margin of the hind wing in both sexes was simply flexed downward to fit under the abdomen. The same margin in many male Kites is reflexed upward over the wing to form a long fold containing scent glands, which emit an odor attractive to females of the species. One can see this organ by examining a male Zebra Swallowtail, whereon it appears as a narrow black fold edged with long, white, hair-like scales. In some species the organ is reduced or absent, but there is always at least a streak visible along the inmost edge of the hind wing to show where it was.

A generalization can be made on the seasons during which members of the genus *Eurytides* are on the wing in Mexico. Eduardo C. Welling points out (in correspondence) that in tropical southern Mexico all species of the genus emerge in the late dry season, from March on, and that almost all of them disappear as the wet season advances, which means that most individuals of all species of *Eurytides* are absent from September on. Most exceptions to this rule occur in nontropical regions farther north and west, where there are flight records into October.

Likewise, a generalization can be made concerning the red pigments which are found in the Kite Swallowtails of genus *Eurytides*. These red pigments belong to type A, which is unlike that of Fluted Swallowtails of the genus *Papilio*, whose pigments are of type B (Ford, 1944). It is the same pigment as that found in the Aristolochia Swallowtails of the genus *Parides*; since some Kites mimic these Aristolochia Swallowtails, they have an initial advantage in the potentially similar red hues. The hues of these red pigments in the genus *Eurytides* range from a brilliant vermilion to a dull, grayed version of the same hue.

THE MARCELLUS GROUP

Taken as a whole this is the northernmost group of Kites, which contains the Zebra Swallowtail, the only member of the genus *Eurytides* commonly found within U.S. borders. Of the ten species in the group, four are found in Mexico and the U.S., three in the West Indies, one in Panama, one in Colombia and Venezuela, and yet another, with a disconnected range, in southeastern Brazil and northern Argentina. Most species are of the black-striped-white Kite configuration.

37. *Eurytides marcellus* (Cramer) 1777

ZEBRA SWALLOWTAIL   Pl. X, Figs. 1,2,3,4

Expanse: 60-90+ mm   **Tails:** 15-27 mm
Description. Sexes similar. All wings with alternating pale and dark stripes; hairs fringing ♂ scent fold white. UnHW with red stripe running parallel to abdomen and bordered with black on *both*

sides. Size, length of tail, and amount of black vary with season (see forms below).

Habitat. Likes open woodlands, or trails through forests, but will also fly in open fields if they are brushy, or around marshes if the food plant grows there. At times it also flies in planted fields, and uncommonly in parks and gardens.

Flight. Late March to mid-October in Washington, D.C.; March to December in Florida. Two to four broods.

Food Plants. Pawpaw (*Asimina triloba* or *A. parviflora*) of family Annonaceae.

Early Stages. Mature larva pea green, with a hump the apex of which is on third segment of thorax where there is a wide black band edged with yellow; on other segments there are narrow cross bands of black and yellow.

Distribution.

Canada: s. Ontario.

U.S.: All of Florida (rare in Keys), northward to New England where rare. Mich.; common in Ind. and Ill.; only a few summer visitors in Wis., where food plant does not grow. One record in Minn.; in Texas it flies in eastern wooded area; common resident in Kan.; in Neb. flies only in se. part.

Mexico: one example from lower Rio Bravo (Rio Grande).

Forms. Studies have shown that the seasonal forms of this species could be reduced to two, with intergrades, but as the three-form division has a long tradition it is given here. Seasonal forms:

f. "marcellus"

First out, small; red spot at anal angle large, tail short with white tip.

f. "telamonides"

Late spring, more black, tails longer and with white border part way.

f. "lecontei"

Summer, larger, tails longer with white border to base, red spot small, and dark markings cover outer half of HW.

A fourth form, "floridensis" (see Pl. X, Fig. 4), was described as a subsp. by Holland; its status and relationship to other forms should be studied.

135

38.   *Eurytides philolaus*   (Boisduval) 1836

DARK ZEBRA SWALLOWTAIL   Pl. X, Figs., 5,6

Expanse: 65-80 mm   **Tails:** 21-23 mm
Description. Sexes sometimes differ. Male: like *E. marcellus* (37), except that it has a broad, straight, black border of even width on
   outer margins of all wings; inside the border, a nearly vertical
   greenish white stripe runs from apex of FW cell to near mid HW.
   Antennae black (brownish yellow in *E. marcellus*). Female pre-
   sents two forms: One form is like ♂. Second form, "niger", is
   nearly all black, except for the two red spots at anal angle and the
   HW submarginal lunules (see Pl. X, Fig. 6).
Habitat. In both temperate and tropical areas, and in either forest trails
   and clearings, or more open fields, pastures and road sides. In El
   Salvador it is limited to under 100 m (330 ft) alt., but in Mexico it
   is found up to at least 700 m (2300 ft).
Flight. This is the first species of the genus to emerge in northern Yuca-
   tan, appearing in late March in incredible numbers; it flies into
   June there. Farther north there is an abundant April brood, fol-
   lowed by a second in July and August.
Food Plants. Species in family Annonaceae.
Early Stages. Described but not published.
Distribution. Mexico: From Yucatan N along e. coast. Rio Blanco and
   Puente Nacional, Veracruz; Valles and El Pujal, San Luis Potosi;
   Tamaulipas. In s. Chiapas; Oaxaca; Mesa de San Diego, Puebla.
   Sierra Madre Oriental. Pacific coast as far N as Nayarit and
   Sinaloa.
   U.S.: One record, Padre Is., Port Isabel, Cameron Co., Texas.

39.   *Eurytides oberthueri*   (Roths. & Jordan) 1906

OBERTHUER'S ZEBRA SWALLOWTAIL   Pl. XII, Fig. 1.

Expanse: 66 mm (one specimen)   **Tails:** 19 mm
Description. The figure on Pl. XII is drawn from a photograph of the
   type; the color is the palest greenish *white*. The light bars in FW
   cells and pale areas in centers of both wings are much wider than
   in *E. philolaus* (38) and FW is semitransparent toward tip. In
   specimens from w. Mexico the light color is said to be yellowish
   white. The type came from Honduras but this rare species is not

listed for that country now. Vazquez brought *oberthueri* to light as a Mexican species in 1953.

Habitat. Tropical forest.

Flight. Only record known to author is for June.

Food Plants and Early Stages. Unknown.

Distribution. Very local, and with a split range. E. Mexico: San Martin, Tuxtla, Veracruz; Yaxchilan, Chiapas, at 150 m (500 ft). In west taken at Coahuayana, in nw. corner of Michoacan on coast; possibly also in neighboring Colima.

40.   *Eurytides epidaus* (Doubleday) 1846

EPIDAUS SWALLOWTAIL   Pl. XII, Figs., 4,6.

Expanse: 70-80 mm   **Tails:** 28-35 mm

Description. Sexes similar. FW transparent in outer half, becoming semitransparent toward base. Black bars in FW cell very narrow, as compared to those of Zebras. *E. epidaus* looks much like members of the Protesilaus group (45, et seq.) but can be discriminated by:

(1)   the red line on UnHW, which has black border on *both* sides, at least at front (in Protesilaus group border is on one side only);

(2)   second black bar of UpHW, which is nearly complete, forming wing-length black V [*E. agesilaus* (45) has inner bar only; *E. protesilaus* (46) has neither, on upper side].

Habitat. Subtropical and tropical; open fields, hedgerows, sunny road sides, recently abandoned *milpas*, and the vicinity of towns, which it will enter to drink from puddles along streets.

Flight. Emerges in April in Yucatan and continues in full force into August, after which it disappears. On the south coast of Oaxaca it is later, emerging in May and June.

Food Plants. *Annona reticulata*, of family Annonaceae. Seems not to oviposit on related *A. muricata*.

Early Stages. Mature larva leaf green, slightly enlarged at thorax, tapering toward abdominal tip (Fig. 9-1a). Yellow collar on first segment; back a velvet green, bordered on sides with narrow yellow rays. The effect of this coloration is to blend caterpillar with leaf. Chrysalis is shown in Fig. 9-1b. Life history described in Ross (1964a).

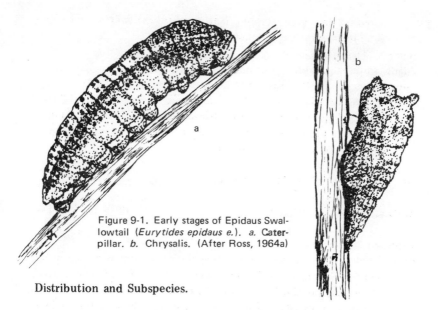

Figure 9-1. Early stages of Epidaus Swallowtail (*Eurytides epidaus e.*). *a.* Caterpillar. *b.* Chrysalis. (After Ross, 1964a)

Distribution and Subspecies.

40.a.   *E. epidaus epidaus* (Doubleday) 1846

Red anal spots bordered with white in front. Distribution: Yucatan, Tabasco and Campeche; n. Chiapas; Tule, Oaxaca, at 1500 m (5000 ft); Veracruz: Rio Blanco, 700 m (2300 ft) Tuxtla Mts., 350 m (1100 ft); Jacala, Hidalgo, 1400 m (4500 ft) and subtropical; Arroyo del Calabezas, San Luis Potosi.

40.b.   *E. epidaus fenochionis*   (Godman & Salvin) 1868

No definite border above anal red spots; these larger than in other two subspecies; UpHW has more extensive black. Distribution: sw. Mexico.; Querétaro, Que.; Progreso, Morelos; Michoacan (Apatzingan and Uruapan); Colima; coast of Guerrero; S of Puebla; Oaxaca.

40.c.   *E. epidaus tepicus* (Roths. & Jordan) 1906

UpHW submarg. spots larger, narrow white border on red anal spots, and tail with extended silvery white. Life history described in Comstock & Vazquez (1960). Distribution: Jalisco; Nayarit; S of Sinaloa.

MIMIC GROUP

There are eighteen species in this Mimic group and, although they are closely related to the Marcellus group, they look nothing like those species. Instead, their appearance has shifted and all are mimics either of Aristolochia Swallowtails, or of the unrelated Heliconids, which are likewise protected, inedible species. Aberrantly, the caterpillars of some Mimic species are dark and tuberculate, which is like the *models* rather than like other members of the genus *Eurytides*. The Mimic group is predominantly South American, but there are four species in Mexico, and three of these are good enough mimics of Mexican *Parides* ♀ to fool both birds and beginners.

Species of this group not only *look* like the models, but also *behave* like them. According to Ross (1967) *E. branchus*, *E. belesis* and *E. phaon* have given up the high, soaring flight which is characteristic of most members of this genus. Instead they fly among hedgerows and close to the ground (at two to four feet) which is the habit of *Parides* species. Both *branchus* and *belesis* have also adopted a slow flight, which is again that of models in the genus *Parides* rather than the swift flight typical of Kite Swallowtails.

To distinguish mimics belonging to the genus *Eurytides* from their models, keep in mind that the mimics have red spots at the *bases of the wings on the underside* (models do not) and mimics have pinkish-red spots on the *thorax* and the *first segment* of the abdomen, but (*E. phaon* excepted) not further down the abdomen nor at the tip. The mimics have only a narrow scent fold in males, while males of the models have a wide back-fold along the inner edge of the hind wing which contains white, cottony material. The chart below, supported by reference to figures, will help discriminate these species.

MIMIC Plate XI		MODEL Plate XIV	
Eurytides branchus,	Fig. 6 :	*Parides iphidamas* ♀,	Fig. 6
Eurytides belesis,	Fig. 3 :	*Parides polyzelus*,	Fig. 3
Eurytides thymbraeus,	Fig. 1 :	*Parides photinus*,	Fig. 1

41. *Eurytides branchus* (Doubleday) 1846

THE BRANCHUS MIMIC   Pl. XI, Fig. 6.

Expanse: 70-80 mm   **Tails:** None

Description. Sexes similar, black, with a cream-colored patch on FW (at apex of discal cell) comprising three spots, with largest spot inside cell. HW has a red band comprising four long, parallel, red bars, plus one irregular red spot at either end of band. Can be distinguished from model by the fact that red bars are separated by black (in model red band is continuous), and by four red spots at base of UnHW.

Habitat. The vicinity of thick woods and (in Tuxtla Mts., Ver.) the margins of semievergreen seasonal forest.

Flight. Records known to author run from April through September.

Food Plants. Doubtless Annonaceae. South American subspecies on Magnoliaceae and Verbenaceae.

Early Stages. Undescribed for Mexican race.

Distribution. Temperate and subtropical areas of the Sierra Madre Oriental. Potrero Nuevo, Veracruz; San Quintin and Comitan, Chiapas; Presidio.

Forms. The f. "belephantes" has no white patch on FW. (Note the reverse counterpart under next species.)

42. *Eurytides belesis* (Bates) 1864

THE BELESIS MIMIC   Pl. XI, Fig. 3.

Expanse: 75-80 mm   **Tails:** None

Description. Sexes similar: black except for white fringe along wing margins, and a red band on HW in form of six submarg. spots. Even the red color is a good match for the ♂ of model, *Parides polyzelus* (55).

Habitat. Borders of secondary and primary forests, and along hedgerows.

Flight. Records known to author run from May through August.

Food Plant. "Guanabana" (*Annona muricata*). This butterfly is the opposite of *E. epidaus* (40) in the choice of food plant, as it does not use the nearby *A. reticulata*.

Early Stages. Young larva has forepart much enlarged into a "false head"; in mature larva this is diminished; velvety black with white saddle on 4th and 5th abdominal segments. The segments bear longitudinal rows of dull-red tubercles. Pupa very unusual: looks like an acorn in a cup and has a 5-mm projecting snout on thorax (Fig. 9-2). Life history described in Ross (1964a).

Distribution. Temperate to tropical areas of Sierra Madre Oriental. Description of early stages came from Catemaco, Tuxtla Mts., Veracruz. Chiapas (Mapastepec and San Quintin). Sierra Madre del Sur and up west coast as far N as Colima and Jalisco.

Forms. The f. "hephaestion" has white patches on FW.

Figure 9-2. **"Acorn"** pupa of The Belesis Mimic (*Eurytides belesis*).

43.   *Eurytides thymbraeus* (Boisduval) 1836

THE THYMBRAEUS MIMIC   Pl. XI, Fig. 1,2.

Expanse: 80-85 mm   **Tails:** 9-13 mm

Description. Sexes similar. Upper surface of wings black with an iridescent blue or green sheen. FW without markings; UpHW with two rows of dull red spots, those in submarg. row are chevron-shaped, inner row arrowhead-shaped. Tails very narrow, and length varies, being shorter in the better mimics. Under surface a perfect mimic of *Parides photinus* (51); upper surface not as exact.

Habitat. Flies in more open country than preceding species. In many localities it flies together with *Parides photinus*.

Flight. Records known to author run from May through October.

Food Plant. *Annona cherimola*, Cherimoya.

Distribution and Subspecies.

43.a.   *E. thymbraeus thymbraeus* (Boisd.)

As described above. Distribution: Sierra Madre Oriental in Veracruz and Chiapas. Also certain places in the mountains of Morelos, Guerrero, and Oaxaca.

43.b.   *E. thymbraeus aconophos* (Gray) 1852

Differs from preceding race by having only one row of red spots, the outer row, on UpHW. Distribution: Valley of the Rio Balsas; Guerrero (Iguala); Morelos (Tepoztlan); Puebla; Oaxaca. Central Mexico: Jalisco; Michoacan (Uruapan); Guanajuato (Celaya). Colima, Nayarit and S of Sinaloa.

44.   *Eurytides phaon* (Boisduval) 1836

THE PHAON MIMIC   Pl. XI, Figs. 4,5.

Expanse: 65-77 mm   **Tails:** None; sometimes short tooth

Description. Sexes similar. Pattern of upper surface cryptic (colored for concealment). Greenish iridescence over all; UpFW with creamy submarg. spots, posterior ones bulbous, anterior ones fading to streaks. UpHW with broad, light-green median band, and a row of minute, cream-green, submarg. dots. Lateral red spots along abdomen.

It is on under surface that good mimicry of *Battus* species has developed. Base color is brown; on HW a brick-red zigzag row around margin; FW with submarg. cream spots; pattern gives a good imitation of *Battus polydamas* (59). Both under and upper surfaces are much like *B. laodamas* (62).

Habitat. Immediate vicinity of woods, and among hedgerows.

Flight. Records known to author run from April through October.

Food Plants. *Annona* spp.

Early Stages. Undescribed.

Distribution. The species ranges as far S as Ecuador and Venezuela. Eastern Mexico: Galeana, Nuevo Leon, 2000 m (6600 ft); Valle and Arroyo del Calabezas, San Luis Potosi; El Sol, Tamazunchale, S.L.P.; Highway between Tampico, Tamaulipas and Pozo Rico, Veracruz; Nautla, Ver.; Tuxtla Mts., Ver., 350 to 500 m (1100 to 1600 ft); Tabasco; pen. of Yucatan; ne. Oaxaca; Chiapas (Mapastepec).

Forms. The f. "eridamas" (Pl. XI, Fig. 5) has a row of red spots replacing green band of UpHW; and f. "xenarchus" has a solid red band. Forms are variable in amount of red: some are good mimics of *Parides polyzelus* (55) on UpHW; others resemble *P. montezuma* (53) on UnHW.

PROTESILAUS GROUP

Members of this group are black-on-white striped Kite Swallowtails that look much like the Epidaus Swallowtail of the Marcellus group, but they are not closely related. There is a simple distinction: members of the Marcellus group have black margins on *both* sides of the red line that runs down the under side of the hind wing; in the Protesilaus group the black border is on only *one* side and, as it happens, the two species described below differ on *which* side of the red. There are nine species in this group, of which only these two are found north of Panama.

45.   *Eurytides agesilaus* (Guerin) 1835

LESSER WHITE PAGE   Pl. XII, Figs. 2,3.

Expanse: 63-70 mm   **Tails:** 21-24 mm

Description. Sexes similar. Greenish-white ground color with longitudinal black stripes. Differs from *E. epidaus* (40) in: FW not transparent, and lack of one broad black band which forms the V on the hind wing of that species. Differs from *E. protesilaus* (46) which has, on upper side, neither band of black V. *E. agesilaus* has the black border on *outer* side of UnHW red line (*protesilaus* has black along *inner* side of red line).

Habitat. Lowlands, including dry thorn bush in w. Mexico, as well as rain forest of e. Mexico. Along sunny roads in Tuxtla Mts., Veracruz.

Flight. In Yucatan this species emerges in May, continues into June, then disappears until a second flight (which may be meager, or very heavy) in September. It emerges in late May to June on the s. coast of Oaxaca. Records from w. Mexico run into October.

Food Plants and Early Stages. Unknown.

Distribution and Subspecies. The species is found in Mexico, then skips to Panama and South America. The two Mexican subspecies intergrade completely and probably should be forms.

45.a.   *Eurytides agesilaus neosilaus* (Hopfer) 1866
                                Pl. XII, Fig. 2.
Pale submarg. band of UpFW wider than dark band standing inside it. Distribution: Sierra Madre Oriental. Veracruz; Tabasco; Campeche; Quintana Roo (X-Can).

45.b.   *E. agesilaus fortis* (Roths. & Jordan) 1906
                                Pl. XII, Fig. 3.
Pale submarg. band of FW not wider than the dark bands. Distribution: Sierra Madre del Sur: Oaxaca; Guerrero (Chilpanzingo);

Salada, Colima. Roths. & Jordan added the Atoyac Valley, Veracruz, for a transitional form, but Hoffmann drops that, making the subspecies purely e. and w.

46.   *Eurytides protesilaus penthesilaus*   (Felder) 1865

NORTHERN WHITE PAGE   Pl. XII, Fig. 5.

Expanse: 80-87 mm   **Tails:** 28-31 mm

Description. Discriminated from similar Mexican species by the fact that there are no black bands forming a V on the *upper* side of the hind wing, although those on the under side show through. The male scent fold is decorated with long, silky white hairs and if the fold is opened a large brush of black hair-like scales will be seen. UnHW red line has black border on *inner* side.

Habitat. Males are hilltoppers, making roaming flights over long stretches of open country or forest; they land only to take moisture from damp sand or puddles. Females presumably seclude themselves in forests as they are never collected.

Flight. Follows the same pattern as the preceding species (45), emerging in late May; a second brood takes it into September.

Food Plants. S. American subspecies on Magnolia and Verbena fams.

Distribution. Sierra Madre Oriental: Veracruz (Orizaba); N of Oaxaca; Tabasco; Yucatan; Chiapas (San Quintin).

Note. A Brazilian scholar makes this Mexican race of a South American species into a full species on its own. There is little evidence for making a decision one way or the other but, whatever its status, the Northern White Page is the most magnificent of the North American Kite Swallowtails. Its black lines and red anal spots are crisply set off, like print on a page, and the white ground has a pearly sheen.

Subspecies.

46.a.   *Eurytides protesilaus penthesilaus*

As described above. (*E. protesilaus protesilaus* is South American.)

46.b.   *Eurytides protesilaus macrosilaus* (Gray) 1852

Has smaller red spots at anal angle, and the black markings are paler. Centered S of our area but reaches Mexico in Quintana Roo and lowland Chiapas.

THYASTES GROUP

This small group of six species, half of which appear in Mexico, retains the triangular shape of the hind wing, and the long, slender tail, but in place of the black-on-white stripes these have a central block of color, with brown or black borders around the wing margins. (*Eurytides thyastes* is South American.)

47. *Eurytides marchandi* (Boisduval) 1836

MARCHAND'S KITE SWALLOWTAIL   Pl. XIII, Fig. 1.

Expanse: 75-80 mm   **Tails:** 18-22 mm
Description. Sexes similar. Median block and submarginal spots a tawny orange. Discal cell of FW brownish black with two orange spots in it. Tail dark with orange border along inner length.
Habitat. Hottest, lowland, tropical rainforests, from Belice (Br. Honduras) across c. and s. El Petén region of Guatemala, into the valley of the Rio Usumacinta, including eastern Chiapas, and into n. Oaxaca where the lowland rainforest enters that state. It is localized in the w. part of its range, which includes the hottest areas of Tabasco and Veracruz.
Flight. Varies but may begin from late March to early May; continues to August, and there are some September records.
Food Plants and Early Stages. Unknown.
Distribution. Veracruz; Tabasco; n. part of Oaxaca and e. Chiapas.

48. *Eurytides lacandones* (Bates) 1864

INDIANS' KITE SWALLOWTAIL   Pl. XIII, Fig. 3.

Expanse: 70-75 mm   **Tails:** 23-25 mm
Description. Sexes similar. Central triangular area of all wings the palest of yellows; tips of tails same color. Borders brown; no light lines crossing dark FW discal cell.
Habitat. Hot lowland rainforests, as for the preceding species (47), but its range is more limited, going no farther W than the valley of the Rio Usumacinta in e. Chiapas.
Flight. Emerging from late March to early May, flying no later than August.
Distribution. S of Veracruz; Tabasco; Chiapas.

49.   *Eurytides calliste* (Bates) 1864

CALLISTE KITE SWALLOWTAIL   Pl. XIII, Fig. 2

Expanse: 60-70 mm   **Tails:** 15-18 mm

Description. Sexes similar. Differs from *E. lacandones* (48) by a bright and cheerful lemon color, and the presence of two yellow lines through the black FW cell. There is also a yellow bar anterior to these and a dotted yellow line to apex of FW. Tail has yellow inner margin and tip.

Habitat. Very different from preceding two species (47,48). *E. calliste* is a montane species flying to 1200 or 1500 m (4000 or 5000 ft). It likes the sandy banks of streams in forested areas, and is one of the few Kite species in which ♂♂ regularly visit the blossoms of flowers.

Flight. Seasonally different from other Kites. In Mexico it emerges as early as Feb. (Jan. in Guatemala), and flies throughout the spring months at high altitudes. Flight continues through June and July.

Food Plants and Early Stages. Unknown.

Distribution. S. and c. Veracruz, Tuxtla Mts., 1250 to 1550 m (4100 to 5100 ft); Tabasco; Campeche; Quintana Roo; Chiapas; Oaxaca, at 1450 m.

DOLICAON GROUP

There is one Mexican species in this seven-member group (*Eurytides dolicaon* is South American), and a possible second species in Guatemala. Members of the group differ from other, nonmimic, Kites by having a rounded rather than triangular hind wing, and the front two veins of the forewing are fused into one, which is rare in American Kites though common in Old World species. This species and the preceding two were first collected by Godman and Salvin on an expedition through Central America in search of birds, reptiles, and fish. Among their collections were 425 species of butterflies, many of which were new to science.

50.   *Eurytides salvini* (Bates) 1864

SALVIN'S KITE SWALLOWTAIL   Pl. XIII, Fig. 4.

Expanse: 75-80 mm   **Tails:** 22-25 mm

Description. Sexes similar. FW projects in a lateral point at the apex (falcate). Ground color white or creamy white, UpFW with black bar through mid-part of discal cell, and a longer one beyond cell which reaches black border of outer margin. No black bars on UpHW. Double red anal spots heavily underlined with black.

Habitat. The hottest lowland tropical rainforests, but range limited as in *E. lacandones* (48), flying no farther than e. Chiapas and s. Tabasco in Mexico.

Flight. Emerges from late March to early May, and flies through June, at least.

Food Plants. A Brazilian member of group on Laurel family.

Distribution. Tabasco and Chiapas (also Guatemala and British Honduras).

10

SOME HOWS AND WHYS OF MIMICRY

Mimicry, which has often been mentioned in this book, is a frequently controversial subject, but there are certain facts which are self-evident. For example, there are species which look not at all like their close relatives but resemble instead, in pattern, shape and color, the butterflies of totally different families, or perhaps the most distant and least related members of their own families. These seemingly eccentric shifts in appearance soon drew the attention of entomologists, for they caused much trouble to those who were classifying these insects. Sometimes a female, which had varied from the male form, would be described as a new species—only to be identified later, by rearing adults from caterpillars, as merely the mate of a species already well known. Or, again, some students placed models and mimics together in the same genus because of mutual resemblance; thus the butterflies fooled even very close observers.

In the 1860's the explorer-naturalist Henry Walter Bates published his studies of mimicry among South American butterflies, including the Papilionids, and the common type of mimicry now bears his name. Any study of Batesian mimicry begins with both *why* and *how* questions on the change of appearance in mimetic butterflies. First of all, one should discard any thought that the butterfly somehow wills a change. The individual insect has no more chance of willing a change in its appearance than the reader has of willing to look like Charles Darwin. What happens is that small changes take place, some of which will be noted later, that initiate a partial resemblance to another species which is for some reason unpalatable to birds and other predators. If there is a minute advantage in the changed appearance, those members of the population which possess the new look will leave more survivors than those which do not and, given enough time, the new character will become fixed in the population. The same sequence of events lies behind any shift toward a cryptic (concealing) coloration, even though the outcome is quite the reverse—hiding rather than calling attention. These changes are not frequent, and mimicry is not widespread among butterflies as a whole, even though Swallowtails worldwide are often involved in mimic/model situations.

For a shift toward mimicry the prime requirement is a model which has proven its distastefulness to predators and is thus protected. Some butterflies have achieved this status, particularly among the Danaids, Heliconids and part of the Papilionid family, and along with the protection they have evolved a special appearance of their own called "warning coloration." There would be no value in being distasteful, or even poisonous, if the predator had to eat the butterfly in order to discover the fact, so these kinds have developed colors, such as red or yellow set against black, to advertise rather than conceal their existence. They often have red spots on the body which are supposed to indicate glands from which poisons might be secreted if the body be crushed. To make sure that their message gets across, these species often develop a lazy, open flight as opposed to the quick darting flight of unprotected species. The slow speed gives the predator plenty of time to think about its potential dinner before lunging for it.

American Swallowtails are provided with just such a model in the Aristolochia Swallowtails of their own family, whose food plant presumably supplies the distasteful element. It could have been very much otherwise, however, as Swallowtails of the African and Indo-Australian regions often mimic regional members of the family to which the Monarch butterfly belongs. Monarchs are presumably made inedible by poisons in the milkweed on which *their* caterpillars feed. Granted that it would be useful to copy some protected species, how does a bright yellow Tiger Swallowtail change? While genetic studies have demonstrated that most of the needed changes take place in minute steps, the American Swallowtails have available one simple and rather large beginning step.

Melanism, as the appearance of dark forms is called, is of common occurrence among many kinds of animals, and once a dark genetic form is established a certain number of, say, black sheep will appear among the light-colored ones. Mimicry in the dark female form of the Eastern Tiger Swallowtail is not much more complicated than that. Black alone can serve the butterfly as warning coloration, as was demonstrated first in predation by chickens and then by tanagers and flycatchers (Brower et al., 1971). The warning works, of course, only if the birds have had some prior experience with dark butterflies which were *inedible*. In Canada, where the model for this instance, the Pipevine Swallowtail, is absent, the female Tiger Swallowtails are all of the yellow form, while in the U.S. the percentage of dark females varies from nearly 0 to as much as 85%, depending upon the abundance of the model in each area. How superficial mimicry really is can be seen in the fact that the normal black "V" pattern is still visible even after the yellow is clouded over with dark scales. The developing mimicry in this case is simplified by the fact that the model also has tails, so there is no need for the mimic to lose them.

One will perhaps remember that the Dark Zebra Swallowtail has an all-black female form on which only the red anal-angle spots show against the black ground, providing a start toward mimicry of any of the red-banded, black species of *Parides*. This black form does retain its tails, but as the presence or absence of tails is under a simple genetic control they may in time be lost. There are a number of Swallowtails in which the male is tailed and nonmimetic while the female is tailless and mimetic, the African *Papilio dardanus* being the most studied example.

Since in both of these examples only the female is involved, it is reasonable to pose a "why"? Why is it often only the female of a species which is involved in mimicking? The first thing to note is that for mimicry to be useful, from the mimic's standpoint, there should be considerably more models than mimics, or the predator will learn the wrong lesson. The probability should be in favor of many birds' having sampled the inedibles early in life and learned to reject them. It also helps if the model be more widely distributed than the mimic, since many of the predatory birds are migratory. In Mexico and Central America the three more common red-on-black models, *Parides photinus* (51), *P. polyzelus* (55) and *P. iphidamas* (56) meet these requirements, and the fact that all of these models share similar patterns reinforces the prevalence of models over mimics.

The advantage to a species wherein only the female is a mimic becomes obvious: there can be twice as many of the mimic species without unduly affecting the apparent numerical ratio between models and mimics. Egg-laying females are in greater danger than males since they must fly slowly in search of the proper food plant and then alight and rest on a leaf while depositing an egg. Further, if a male does fall victim to a predator it has little or no effect on the future of the species, while the loss of a female which has not completed egg laying is serious. Since the advantages of a sex-limited mimicry are apparent, it is fair to ask why both sexes are so often involved in mimicry, and there is no ready answer. It may be noted as possibly relevant that female Swallowtails have more variant forms than do males, quite apart from whether or not they are mimics. E.B. Ford makes a suggestion based on butterfly courtship behavior, in which consent is a female choice. Visual stimuli are important in this decision, and Ford surmises that males with normal markings are more successful in stimulating the female to copulate than are males with variant and less familiar patterns. Males, on the other hand, are not hesitant and do not make individual decisions. The outcome of this difference in behavior would be selection for standard visual characters in males, but no such pressure against variation of female patterns. Certainly the ability to vary is important in incipient mimicry, and species differ in whether one or both sexes show this potential.

There is a second kind of mimicry, (described by F. Müller). The essence of Müllerian mimicry is that the two or even more species involved in the association are equally unpalatable to predators, so the relationship is not one of the weak hiding under the protection of the strong, as in Batesian mimicry. It is instead an association of protected species in which the advantage derives from simple arithmetic and is thus easy to grasp: there is a safety in numbers which derives from merely dividing any risk. This idea, which lies behind every insurance policy, applies equally to butterflies. When several species of *Parides*, or *Battus*, which are already protected by their unpalatability, fly together in the same area they share in this protection of numbers as well. Although they are inedible, birds or other predators will have to learn this truth in each generation and in that process some butterflies will be killed, even if not eaten. When more than one species is involved each species loses fewer members than it otherwise would, to the advantage of each species. As the species are relatives to begin with, they already look much alike, and the selective pressure will serve to increase the homogeneity of the group of species. The essential requisite is that they fly together, and even in this they are aided by having similar habitat preferences, so all that is required is that each species find a slightly different ecological niche.

A curious sidelight of numerical protection is that it affords a much greater shield to rare, and therefore weak species, than to associated species which are abundant. For those who are mathematically inclined, the proportional advantage for each of two species is as the *squares* of their relative numbers. Thus, if two associated species exist in a ratio of 1 : 5, the protective advantage to the lesser and weaker will be 25 : 1, which is quite an umbrella for a species that might be endangered because of its low numbers..

There is also another aspect of numerical protection which has received little study but is of great interest. It is based on the fact that these same principles apply to associations in which all members are perfectly edible and unprotected. The Mimetic group of Kite Swallowtails is one such potential association and the Anchisiades group of Fluted Swallowtails is another. Whenever mixed groups from the above genera fly together they share losses, quite apart from any protection given them by models in the genus *Parides*, with which they also mingle at times.

The few thoughts presented above are scarcely an introduction to the complex subject of mimicry, but perhaps they will suggest projects to students who may thus increase available information. It may be noted that while mimicry of the Pipevine Swallowtail by several U.S. species has been studied in detail, no work has been published on the more complex groups of mimics and models in Mexico. Very fine work on both Batesian and Müllerian mimicry, involving some of the same species, has been done in Costa Rica by Young (1971). Study, using the same capture-mark-recapture method for assessing such relationships, is much needed for the Mexican region. Until that is undertaken all one knows is that *Eurytides thymbraeus* (43) does fly with *Parides photinus* (51), and that both inhabit the same general areas as *Papilio anchisiades* (27). Beyond that one is reasoning from analogy with other regions.

THE ARISTOLOCHIA SWALLOWTAILS

Genus **Parides** Hübner 1819

Genus **Battus** Scopoli 1777

Members of this division are united by a common choice of larval food plants, the alkaloid-bearing vines and shrubs of the genus *Aristolochia*, of which dutchman's pipe and Virginia snakeroot are examples. Occasionally their caterpillars are found on plants of other families, but their safety from predators derives from these toxic plants. The genus *Parides* has about 46 species in the American tropics, and another 29 or so in the Indo-Australian and Oriental regions. Most species are predominantly black, many with red or red and white markings. Some American members also display brilliant greens and blues. Old World species tend to be large and drab, while American species are medium to small in size. The genus *Battus* is limited entirely to the New World and comprises 14 species, some of which, such as our Pipevine Swallowtail, show iridescent blue-greens, while others have a bronzy-green ground color of considerable richness.

11

THE INEDIBLES

THE CATTLE HEARTS
Genus **Parides** Hübner 1819

Members of the genus *Parides* are called "Cattle Hearts" in Latin America, presumably because of the blood-red spots, which are often tapering in shape. The females of some species are very different from their males, and often females of two different species are confusingly alike. Fortunately the only pair of female look-alikes in Mexico can be separated by the color of their fringe spots. They might be confused with their mimics, but it may be remembered that the Kite mimics have red spots *at the bases of the wings on the under surface*, while the Cattle Hearts have red spots on the *thorax* and along the *abdomen*. Both Cattle Hearts and Gold Rims (genus *Battus*) have scent glands associated with these abdominal red (or yellow) spots, and these emit an acrid odor if the butterfly is in any way pinched.

The genus *Parides* is characterized by *brilliant* red pigments ranging from scarlet through vermilion to orange. The full range of this gradation may be observed in a collection of specimens of the *same species*, for instance *P. polyzelus* (55).

While the red in *Parides* is contributed by a variable *pigment*, its hue is further varied by an iridescence which is of *structural* origin: each scale' is layered, giving interference of light colors which at a near-zero angle of incidence suffuses the red with an increasing tincture of spectral blue, at maximum completely masking the red. This structural iridescence may be general over both fore and hind wings, including the black areas, as in *P. photinus* (51), or it may be confined to the red spots alone, as in *P. polyzelus* (55) and *P. iphidamas* (56).

The male scent fold along the abdominal margin of UpHW (absent in females) is much more prominent and more broadly folded over in *Parides* than in *Eurytides*, and it contains cottony scales inside the fold. This 'cotton' is white in all but the last species, *P. arcas* (57), so if the specimen is a male it is simple to turn back the fold and see if white cotton is present. The genus *Parides* contains three groups which are easily separated: the Ascanius group has submarginal spots on hind wings and at least short tails; the Aeneas group is tailless and has *white* fringe spots along outer margins of both fore and hind wings; the Lysander group is tailless and has *red* fringe spots on margins of hind wings.

ASCANIUS GROUP

This eleven-member group is named for a Brazilian species which is probably the most beautiful example of the genus *Parides*. The species are evenly distributed in the tropical Americas, and Mexico has three representatives.

51.   *Parides photinus*   (Doubleday) 1844

RED AND BLUE CATTLE HEART   Pl. XIV, Fig. 1.

Expanse: 65-80 mm   **Tails:** 5-6 mm (tooth on next inmost vein)
Description. Sexes similar. Ground color of both wings an iridescent blue. White fringe spots on both wings; edge of HW deeply scalloped and with red submarginal crescents, plus an inner row of seven rounded scarlet spots.
     Eurytides thymbraeus (43) is a good mimic of this species but has a longer, thinner tail, and of course red spots at the base of the UnHW.
Habitat. Prefers forest margins and trails and seldom flies in open places. Ross (1964b) noted that in Veracruz they stayed in tropical forest

and did not enter pine woods of the same mountain. Flies from sea level to 2000 m (6600 ft).

Flight. Flies slowly and within four feet of the ground, unless disturbed. Records known to author run from March through September.

Food Plants. *Aristolochia asclepiadifolia. A. grandiflora* in El Salvador.

Early Stages. Egg is shaped like a mushroom (Fig. 11-1), being a fluted cap set on a stem. Ground color of larva in early stages is an orangish red, with a cream-colored saddle on 3rd and 4th abdominal segments. Mature larva velvety black. Most tubercles red, and these are shorter than on larva of genus *Battus*, longest ones being length of segment. Desc. in Ross (1964b).

Distribution. Species flies from Mexico to Costa Rica. Temperate and tropical regions of s. Mexico and along both coasts, Chiapas to Veracruz. Morelos (Cuernavaca), Guerrero; Michoacan; Colima; Jalisco. In many places abundant.

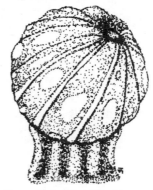

Figure 11-1. Egg of *Parides photinus.* (After Ross 1964b)

Forms. f. "escalantei". Although this was originally described by Hoffmann as a ♀ form, Dr. Escalante, who supplied a photograph of the type specimen, notes that it applies to both sexes, the ♂ having fewer spots. This form is characterized by a row of six submarginal spots on UpFW, beginning at outer angle of wing and arcing inward. Their color is an off-white washed with a light red. All specimens have been collected in the Santa Rosa area of Chiapas, Mexico.

52.   *Parides alopius* (Godman & Salvin) 1890

ALOPIUS CATTLE HEART   Pl. XIII, Fig. 5.

Expanse: 70-80 mm   **Tails:** 8-10 mm, spatulate.

Description. Sexes similar. Wings less glossy blue than in *P. photinus* (51), and appear black. HW with slightly chevron-shaped submarginal lines, of which the posterior three are red, anterior two white. An inner row of minute white dots, except one at anal angle red; ♀ notably larger than ♂.

Habitat. Mountains of western Mexico.
Flight. Records known to author run from May through October.
Food Plants. *Aristolochia* spp.?
Early Stages. Unknown.
Distribution. Chihuahua; Jalisco (Guadalajara and Tepatitlan); Guerrero; Morelos at 1500 m (5000 ft). Uncommon.

53.　　*Parides montezuma* (Westwood) 1842

MONTEZUMA CATTLE HEART　　　　　　　　　　Pl. XIV, Fig. 2.

Expanse: 58-78 mm　　　　　　**Tails:** 3-5 mm, straight and broad.
Description. Female notably larger than ♂, and red spots thicker. Wings black, with narrow white fringe spots. HW with 5 to 7 red submarginal spots, those nearest tail chevron-shaped. No inner row of spots.

　　Eurytides belesis (42) is a good mimic of both this species and the ♂ of *Parides polyzelus* (55). *E. phaon* f. "eridamas" (44) is a perfect mimic on underside.
Habitat. Another woodland species inhabiting both temperate and tropical forests to an elevation of 2000 m (7000 ft) in Mexico. In Tuxtla Mts., Ver., it is most common in recently abandoned cultivated fields, from 300 to 600 m (1000 to 2000 ft) altitude. Males and ♀♀ fly together, taking nectar from flowers.
Flight. Records from April through October.
Food Plants. *Aristolochia* spp. *A. grandiflora* in El Salvador.
Early Stages. No description located.
Distribution. Mexico to Nicaragua. Mexico: from Yucatan N along east coast as far as Tamaulipas. Specifically: Tuxpan, Ver.; Valles, El Pujal, El Bañito, S.L.P.; in S at Cuernavaca, Morelos. Valley of Rio Balsas. Puerto Vallarta, Jalisco.

AENEAS GROUP

　　This is a predominantly South American group of more than two dozen species, mostly tailless and without submarginal spots, although the median band is sometimes set out toward margins of hind wings. The fringe markings are white.

54.   *Parides sesostris zestos* (Gray) 1852

ZESTOS CATTLE HEART   Pl. XIII, Fig. 6.

Expanse: 75-85 mm   **Tails:** None
Description. Sexes differ. Male: glossy black with three iridescent
   green patches on UpFW from inner margin forward, middle spot
   largest, upper one diamond shaped; all three are outside of discal
   cell. UpHW with elongate red spot along scent fold. Female:
   larger, no green. UpFW has buffy-white patches near apex of cell.
   UpHW with partial median band of red spots (anterior ones are
   dots).
Habitat. Tropical forest. In Tuxtla Mts., Ver., from sea level to 500 m
   (1600 ft); this includes lower montane rain forest, semievergreen
   seasonal forest, littoral and swamp woodland. In British Honduras,
   in both secondary and advanced forests where their flyways are
   trails in places where these are wide enough for sunlight to reach
   the forest floor, they fly with *Parides iphidamas* (56) and *Parides
   arcas mylotes* (57), three to five feet above the ground, and are
   attached to separate colonies at half-mile to one-mile intervals.
Flight. Records known to the author run from July through October.
Food Plants. *Aristolochia* spp.
Early Stages. (Based on Brazilian subspecies.) Young larva is a deep
   maroon color, which becomes glossy black in mature caterpillar.
   The tubercles on back of mature larva are thick and blunt. Eggs
   are laid singly.
Distribution. This subspecies from Mexico to Costa Rica; others in
   South America. In e. Mexico: Quintana Roo; Campeche; Tabasco;
   Chiapas; Veracruz (Dos Amates and Coatzacoalcos).
Note. Hoffmann (1940b) lists two species which would be placed here,
   Parides childrenae and *P. lycimenes*. Professional collectors say
   that these two do not cross from Guatemala into Mexico. Students
   might keep a watch for them in e. Chiapas. *P. childrenae* resembles *P. s. zestos*, but has a fourth green spot, within cell; *P.
   lycimenes* has an olive-green, noniridescent patch on FW of male.

55.   *Parides polyzelus* (Felder) 1865

POLYZELUS CATTLE HEART   Pl. XIV, Fig. 3.

Expanse: 70-75 mm (63 mm in subsp. *trichopus*).   **Tails:** None

Description. Sexes similar. Wings black with white fringe spots; UpHW
with five or six elongate red spots which are broader, longer and
paler in ♀; these white, washed pink on UnHW.

The mimic of this species, *Eurytides belesis* (42), is a good
copy of the ♂.

Habitat. A forest species like *P. s. zestos* (54), but flies in temperate as
well as tropical areas. In Tuxtla Mts., Ver., flies in seasonal forest,
lower montane rain forest, littoral and swamp woodland, and
along hedgerows, from sea level to 600 m (2000 ft). Altitudes
given for El Salvador are between 600 and 1100 m (2000 and
3500 ft).

Flight. Flight is weak and close to the ground. Records known to
author run from March through October.

Food Plants. *Aristolochia* spp.

Early Stages. Unknown.

Distribution and Subspecies. Species ranges from Mexico to Honduras.

55.a. *P. polyzelus polyzelus* (Felder)

As described above. Distribution: X-Can, Quintana Roo; Chiapas;
Veracruz (Tuxtla Mts.). Sierra Madre del Sur as far as Oaxaca and
Guerrero.

55.b. *P. polyzelus trichopus* (Roths. & Jordan) 1906

The spots of this subsp. are considerably larger and longer, placing
band nearer margin and making it a nearly solid band. Distribution: w. Mexico: Valley of Rio Balsas; coastal Guerrero; Michoacan; Colima (Comala); Jalisco; Nayarit.

56. *Parides iphidamas iphidamas* (Fabricius) 1793

IPHIDAMAS CATTLE HEART   Pl. XIV, Figs. 5,6.

Expanse: 65-70 mm   **Tails:** None

Description. Sexes differ, but both have black wings with white fringe
spots. Male: FW has a gray-green patch in center of wing, with
white spots in upper end of patch. HW red band narrower and
brighter than on female. Female: FW has a series of white spots
forming a band across more than half of wing at apex of cell.

Habitat. A common insect of both temperate and tropical forests, in which it forms localized colonies which fly with other species of the genus. In Tuxtla Mts., Ver., from sea level to 700 m (2300 ft), in lower montane rain forest, seasonal forest, littoral and swamp woodland. In El Salvador it flies from sea level to 1400 m (4500 ft), being most common between 60 and 1100 m (200 and 3500 ft).
Flight. Records known to author run from March through mid-October.
Food Plant. *Aristolochia grandiflora.*
Early Stages. Three broods in El Salvador, but no descr. of larva found.
Distribution. From Mexico to Panama. In Mexico: Chiapas ("Santa Anita") 800 m (2700 ft), "Irlanda", 1100 m (3500 ft). As far N as central Veracruz (Cotaxtla). In W: Sierra Madre del Sur as far as Guerrero. There are sea level records in Mexico. Other subspecies range south of Panama.

LYSANDER GROUP

This is a small group of eight South American species, one of which has subspecies in Central America and Mexico. *Parides arcas mylotes* is the only member of the genus to reach the U.S. border, and that only on the rarest of occasions. All species in this group have red fringe spots along margins of hind wings, which serve as identifying marks for the group.

57. *Parides arcas mylotes* (Bates) 1861

MYLOTES CATTLE HEART Pl. XIV, Fig. 4.

Expanse: ♂: 60-70 mm, ♀: 68-73 mm **Tails:** None
Description. Sexes differ. Male: FW triangular in shape, with a triangular green patch alongside outer edge of cell, capped by a round white spot; small white and green spot in apex of cell. A red patch rather than a band on UpHW, with red extending well into cell. Female: very similar to *Parides iphidamas* ♀ (56), but the red HW fringe spots distinguish *arcas*. *Eurytides branchus* (41) is a good mimic of the female, but lacks red fringe spots.
Habitat. Tropical and subtropical forests. In Tuxtla Mts., Ver., inhabits the lower forests from sea level to 800 m (2700 ft). Hoffmann (1933) notes it in Soconusco district of w. Chiapas at 25 m and

800 m (85 ft and 2700 ft). In El Salvador it flies from sea level to 1500 m (5000 ft).

Flight. Flight is rapid and close to ground on sunlit portions of trails. Mexican records known to author run March through October. Flies year around in El Salvador and Costa Rica, with four or five broods.

Food Plant. *Aristolochia grandiflora.*

Early Stages. Described in Young (1973).

Distribution. Species: Mexico to Colombia, Venezuela, and the Guianas. This subspecies, from Mexico to Costa Rica. Mexico: Veracruz as far N as Cordoba; Tuxtla Mts., and Ojo d'Agua at 500 m (1600 ft) in hills above Atoyac Valley, Veracruz. Pichucalco, Chiapas; w. Chiapas in Soconusco region. Presumably Tabasco.?

THE GOLD RIMS

Genus **Battus** Scopoli 1777

There are several small genera which are related to *Parides*, two of them comprising the famous Birdwings of the Indo-Australian region, which are the largest and in their own way the most colorful of butterflies. In the New World, *Battus* is the only genus closely related to *Parides*, and it departs from the norm of that genus more than do other related genera. The theory is that this genus branched off from the main stem of Aristolochia Swallowtails in the very distant past. By good fortune the differences between *Battus* and *Parides* are such as even a beginner can recognize with ease.

In *Battus* males the scent scales within the fold along the abdominal margin of the hind wing are never cottony in texture, and they are not white. There are never red bands across the middle of the hind wing in either sex and, except for the Polydamas Gold Rim (59), there are no red spots along the abdomen. When red marks do occur they are of a different pigment and have a *dull* red color—the pigment is the same as that found in the genus *Papilio*, and is chemically unlike that of *Parides* and *Eurytides*. The genus *Battus* is characterized by red pigment of a dull vermilion (brick red) hue in the lunules near the margin of the under surface of the hind wing. The apparent hue is slightly affected by a general (lamellar) iridescence of the scales which contributes varying amounts of spectral blue, depending on the angle of illumination and the angle of view. Most of the spots on the head, abdomen and thorax of *Battus* species are cream, often with a greenish cast, or yellow. *B. polydamas* shows a single red spot at base of UnHW.

Caterpillars as well as adults differ: in *Parides* the tubercles are short and fleshy, while most species in *Battus* have both short and long tubercles. The two behind the head are long, tentacle-like and project forward. Female butterflies of the genus *Battus* lay their eggs in clusters of five or more, so the larvae are found in small gregarious groups.

Figure 11-2. Caterpillar of Pipevine Swallowtail (*Battus philenor*).

The Pipevine Swallowtail is the only tailed member of the genus *Battus* on the mainland, though there is a tailed species in Cuba, and another in Haiti. The Pipevine Swallowtail (58) itself has a form which is both tailless and dwarf. In South America there are several species, including *B. polydamas* (59), which fit the popular name of "Gold Rims", so that name has been retained here for the tailless members of the genus.

58.   *Battus philenor* (L.) 1771

PIPEVINE SWALLOWTAIL   Pl. XV, Fig. 1.

Expanse: 70-85 mm is common; to 100+ mm   **Tails:** 7-10 mm; or none
Description. Sexes similar. Wings dark, with blue- to-green iridescence on UpHW, especially in ♂; ♀ much less iridescent on upper surface. Fringe spots and submarg. spots white, and small on upper surface. UnHW: outer half iridescent blue, with a marginal row of light spots and a curving, submarg. row of round orange spots margined in black.
    Its mimic, the Spicebush Swt. (18), has a round orange spot on forward edge of HW on *upper surface*. The Black Swt. (2) is a fair mimic on *under surface*, but not above.

Habitat. Meadows, open woods, fields, orchards, and gardens. In California, where its native food plant grows along streams and rivers, it is limited to their neighborhoods, except for those occasionally found on garden pipevine. Adults spend much of their time about flower blossoms: fruit tree blossoms, lilac, butterfly bush, clover, and thistles.

Flight. In the South some adults winter over; first emergence in s. Georgia is during warm periods in Jan. and Feb., but in Mar. farther north. On the other hand, they fly through Oct. as far N as Washington, D.C., in favorable years. The later broods produce larger individuals, the outsized ones usually occurring in the late summer brood.

Food Plants. The various species of *Aristolochia:*

> *A. serpentaria*, Virginia snakeroot.
>
> *A. macrophylla*, pipevine.
>
> *A. californica*, dutchman's pipe.
>
> *A. longiflora*, etc.

Curiously, females will lay eggs on *A. elegans*, but the larvae die on this species.

Also reported on:

Asarum spp., wild ginger.

Polygonum spp., knotweed.

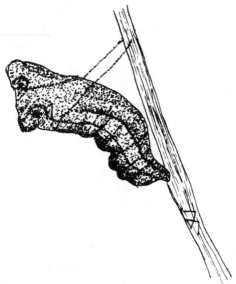

Figure 11-3. Chrysalis of Pipevine Swallowtail (*Battus philenor*).

Early Stages. Mature larva dark purplish brown, with rows of fleshy tubercles the first pair of which points forward; the posterior tubercles are longer than others on abdomen (Fig. 11-2). Chrysalis shown in Fig. 11-3.
Distribution and Subspecies.

58.a. *Battus philenor philenor* (L)

As described above. Distribution: General in Florida, except extreme S; common throughout Georgia, and as far north as Bar Harbor, Maine, but rare in New England; records in s. Ontario, Canada. Gulf states, to Texas: if a slack line be drawn from Dallas to El Paso, Texas, it flies to the south and east of that line. Found throughout Indiana and Illinois, sparse in s. Wisconsin, only two records in Neb. and uncommon in e. Kansas. (*Not* in Minn., the Dakotas, Wyoming, nor Utah.) A few records on domestic pipe-vine in Colorado; single records from central mts. of New Mexico, and spotty in Arizona. (*Not* in Wash. and Oregon.) In s. Calif. only strays from E and S. Much of Mexico.

58.b. *Battus philenor hirsuta* (Skinner) 1908

Smaller and hairy-bodied. An uncertain subsp., perhaps a spring form, as these characters appear outside Calif. In n. Calif. follows food plant: from Shasta Co. S along foothills of Sierra Nevada as far as Millerton Lake, Fresno Co. A second arm travels S along inner Coast Range to San Francisco Bay. Not in Monterey Co., the s. outpost of food plant.

58.c. *Battus philenor acauda* (Oberthuer) 1879 Pl. XV, Fig. 1b.

Dwarf and tailless. Should be a form, as it is occasional in the U.S., fairly common Veracruz and Yucatan, and dominant on Tres Marias Is., Mexico.

59. *Battus polydamas* (L.) 1758

POLYDAMAS GOLD RIM   Pl. XV, Fig. 2.

Expanse: 75-100 mm   **Tails:** None

Description. Sexes similar. Upper surface of wings dark, with silky greenish iridescense to HW in some lights. Outer margin of FW concave; submarg. spots of both wings golden yellow, larger on HW. UnHW with a submarg. row of wavy red marks; anal spot a red bar surmounted by black line, then cream line.

Habitat. Open fields, gardens, and borders of secondary vegetation; seems to fly only in cut-over land with partial clearings. Everywhere both sexes are frequent visitors to flowers, including those of city gardens. In Tuxtla Mts., Ver., common from sea level to 800 m (2700 ft)—not found at higher altitudes. In El Salvador it is common from sea level to 1800 m (6000 ft).

Flight. In Texas, flies from March to December; in Florida from May to November; year around in tropics.

Food Plants. *Aristolochia pentandra, A. macrophylla, A. ringens*, etc. In Texas, larva feeds on *A. elegans*, but not on *A. longiflora*; in Mexico, on *A. asclepiadifolia*.

Early Stages. Mature larva black or brown-yellow; a pair of long fleshy tubercles borne on first segment of thorax; these orange-red and black at base (subsp. *p. lucayus*), or brown-yellow (subsp. *p. polydamas*). Body with four rows of short, orange tubercles. [Comstock & Vazquez (1960) have illus. and descr.]

Distribution. In Florida common south of a line drawn from Tampa to Daytona Beach; n. limit is a line drawn from Cross City to Gainesville to Palataka. Only strays found to N of that line and in Georgia. Local in Gulf states. A colony in Baxter Co., Arkansas; others in Bexar (San Antonio) and Comal Cos., Texas. Hoffmann lists all of Mexico, but it is not found in Baja California and probably not in nw. deserts.

Subspecies. The current view is that *B. p. polydamas* is Cuban and Mexican, while the race found in the U.S. is *p. lucayus*. The latter has broader yellow bands, with UnHW paler, and white bar over anal red bar larger; red submarg. spots also larger.

60.   *Battus eracon*   (Godman & Salvin) 1897

GODMAN'S GOLD RIM   Pl. XV, Fig. 3.

Expanse: 90-110 mm; type was 127 mm   **Tails:** None

Description. Sexes similar, but ♀ much larger. Base color dark bronzy-greenish, UpFW with four to seven buff submarg. spots, becoming faint toward apex; UpHW with submarg. row of buff dots, then inner row of larger greenish spots. UnHW with submarg. row of buffy-white spots, then the inner row of red bars; these red bars separated by blue patches. The HW in some more scalloped along margins than shown in the plate, which portrays the type.

Habitat. Open country, and apparently streamside in tropical deciduous forest. The site at Apatzingan has leguminous and other thorn-studded trees mixed with other growth. It also flies directly on the coast in Jalisco and Guerrero.

Flight. Records known to author run from August through September.

Food Plants. *Aristolochia* spp.

Early Stages. Unknown.

Distribution. SW. Mexico: Jalisco (Puerto Vallarta); Colima (Comala); Michoacan (Apatzingan); coastal Guerrero. Uncommon and local.

Note. Flies with *B. polydamas* (59) and *B. laodamas procas* (62), forming a Müllerian association of greater benefit to the rarer *B. eracon* (see Ch. 10).

61.   *Battus belus varus* (Kollar) 1850

BELUS VARUS GOLD RIM   Pl. XV, Fig. 4.

Expanse: 85-95 mm   **Tails:** None

Description. Sexes differ slightly. Wings bronzy green; outer margin of FW straight. Male: UpHW has median row of greenish-cream bars, the upper one deep and broad, others diminishing in size. Long black hairs on scent fold; upper side of abdomen light yellow, claspers black. Female: four cream submarg. spots on FW; UpHW with zig-zag light submarg. line in addition to median bars. Upper side of abdomen black.

Best distinction from *B. laodamas* (62): on UnHW between margin and red submarg. line there is a row of white dots in *B. belus* (lacking in *B. laodamas*).

Habitat. This species likes sunshine and edges of woods, where it feeds at blossoms. In Tuxtla Mts., Ver., in margins of pine-oak covered ravines, from 200 to 400 m (700 to 1400 ft) altitude.

Flight. Records known to author run May through July.

Food Plants. *Aristolochia* spp.

Early Stages. Larvae gregarious. Larva is black to final stage, then turns maroon, streaked with black. Tubercles on each segment, those behind head much like horns of a snail.

Distribution and Subspecies.

61.a.   *Battus belus varus*

As described. This subspecies ranges from Mexico to Ecuador and Venezuela.   Mexico: Chiapas; Tabasco; s. Veracruz; Oaxaca (region of Isthmus).

61.b.   *B. belus chalceus*   (Roths. & Jordan) 1906

Differs in having UpHW median bars cream white and an extra red mark at top of submarg. spots on UnHW. W. Mexico: Guerrero.

62.   *Battus laodamas*   (Felder) 1859

LAODAMAS GOLD RIM   Pl. XV, Fig. 5.

Expanse: 90-105 mm   **Tails:** None

Description.   Sexes similar but, as for other Gold Rims, *B. polydamas* (59) excepted, there is a sexual difference in color of abdomen. Wings iridescent green; outer margin of FW slightly concave. Both sexes have light submarg. spots on UpFW. Bars in median band of UpHW do not diminish as much as in *B. belus varus* (61). Back of abdomen is cream in ♂, and black in ♀.

Habitat.   Margins of woods, females ovipositing in dense underbrush. Comstock mentions that *B. laodamas procas* ventures near the town of Puerto Vallarta. Collected in pastures near Lake Catemaco, Veracruz, at 300 m (1000 ft) altitude.

Flight.   Records known to author run from May through September.

Food Plants.   *Aristolochia* spp.

Early Stages.   Mature larva is black, the head shiny, the body velvety. First tubercle has black base and a mixture of bright reddish toward tip; the other tubercles are shaded with red their full length. First pair project forward well beyond head. Described in Comstock & Vazquez 1960.

Distribution and Subspecies.

62.a.   *B. laodamas copanae*   (Reakirt) 1863

As described above. E. Mexico: s. and c. Veracruz; Tabasco; Campeche; Yucatan Pen.; n. Chiapas. Oaxaca (?).

62.b.   *B. laodamas procas* (Godman & Salvin) 1890

In this subspecies the median band of HW passes through cell; red submarg. spots of UnHW larger. W. Mexico: Nayarit; Jalisco (Puerto Vallarta); Colima; Michoacan; Guerrero. Oaxaca (?).

63.   *Battus lycidas* (Cramer) 1777

LYCIDAS GOLD RIM   Pl. XV, Fig. 6.

Expanse: 90-95 mm   **Tails:** None

Description. Sexes alike, except back of abdomen is cream in male, and green in female; yellow streak of UpHW shorter in female. Wings iridescent blue-green; dark in UpFW cell; outer margin of FW straight. UpHW with broad primrose-yellow band along abdominal margin—same below. Usually at least anterior small cream spot of a median row present on UpHW, and sometimes faint additional marks.

Habitat. This species likes open spaces, bright sunshine, and water courses.

Flight. Records known to author are from July to August.

Food Plants. *Aristolochia* spp.

Early Stages. Mature larva is a pale glossy gray; the shorter tubercles on back are a dark maroon, the longer ones a pale pink. Behind the head are lateral tubercles which point forward, as with other *Battus* species.

Distribution. The species flies from Mexico to Bolivia and has no subspecies. Mexico: s. and c. Veracruz; Tabasco; Chiapas; Oaxaca.

II

ANCIENT RELATIVES

Subfamily PARNASSIINAE

All of the butterflies discussed in preceding chapters have been True Swallowtails, of the subfamily Papilioninae. In the following chapter we come upon three species which belong to an older branch of the family. All of these are of medium size, without tails, and look very little like what we think of as a Swallowtail butterfly. They do belong to the Swallowtail Family, however, as their larvae have the scent horn (*osmeterium*), and adults possess the small spur (*epiphysis*) on the tibia of the foreleg.

12

EARLY SWALLOWTAILS

Genus **Parnassius** (Fabr.) Latreille 1804

The subfamily Parnassiinae includes some 50 species, all limited to the Northern Hemisphere, and of these nearly 40 belong to the genus *Parnassius*. While species of some other genera in the subfamily have tails and look like 'Swallowtails', the Parnassians are all tailless, but, like the True Swallowtails, they have only one anal vein in each hind wing. On a simpler level, all members of the genus *Parnassius* have a common "style", so that once any species is known all of the others are recognizable as fellow Parnassians.

The wings of Parnassians are most often white or grayish white, sometimes partly transparent; but the first species listed (64) is exceptional in having a yellow ground color in the male. All of our species have target-like rings, on the hind wing at least, which consist of black circles with (usually) red centers, though these centers may be yellow, orange, or white, or even solid black. Abdomens of males are hairier than those of females, and in one case of a different color. Once a female is bred she carries a seal (*sphragis*), which has been secreted by the male, on the lower tip of her abdomen. This effectively prevents further fertilization, and provides the student with a means for identification (Fig. 12-1).

Most of the Parnassians are Eurasian in distribution, but there are three species in northern and western North America. The first of these

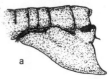
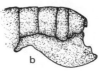
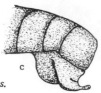

Figure 12-1. Shapes of genital seal (*sphragis*). *a. P. clodius.
b. P. eversmanni. c. P. phoebus.*

is a subspecies, with most of its relatives in Siberia. The second is a full species and purely American and has obviously been on this side of Bering Strait for a very long time, even though its ancestors were probably Asian. The third species is found from the Maritime Alps of Europe across Asia and into southern Alaska and the western mountains of the United States.

These American species are easy enough to discriminate, but there are a number of subspecies and forms which make matters difficult. Parnassians are no distance fliers, and as they live in rugged habitats populations within each species tend to become isolated. When there is no back-and-forth gene flow within the species the isolated pockets begin to differentiate, eventually becoming subspecies. At present there are a great number of described populations or forms, and all that can be done here is to list the best known of these names along with the localities where they were collected. A student can temporarily use locality as the basis for classification, making amendments as his knowledge and collection of specimens grow.

64. *Parnassius eversmanni thor* Hy Edwards 1881

ALASKAN PARNASSIAN   Pl. XVI, Figs. 1,2.

Expanse: 48-58 mm   **Tails:** None

Description. Sexes differ. Male: wings with yellow ground color. UpFW has black-speckled base and two bars in cell; transparent outer areas. UpHW with two black-bordered, circular red spots, one at middle of forward edge, second centered. UnHW has a red bar in addition to spots. Female: ground color whitish, dark areas as above; spots and bar are pink. UnHW with pinkish-red spots at base.

     Antennae of both sexes black. Male has abundant, fine yellow hair on head, thorax, and abdomen.

Habitat. Open fields in mountains of Alaska.

Flight. June and July.

Food Plants. *Corydalis gigantea*, family Fumariaceae. The genus is a close relative of *Dicentra*: dutchman's breeches.

Early Stages. A Parnassian larva is flattened, and it pupates among the litter on the ground. The color of the caterpillar is black, with dark velvety down and yellow spots.

Distribution. The ssp. *thor* flies in the Yukon drainage; Seward Peninsula; North Slope to n. edge of Brooks Range foothills, (but not Arctic Coastal Plain); Denali Hwy. on s. side of Alaska Range. Mt. Headley, near New Aiyansh, B.C., above timberline at 6400 ft; the latter is south of previous records.

65.   *Parnassius clodius* Ménétriés 1855

CLODIUS PARNASSIAN   Pl. XVI, Figs. 5,6.

Expanse: 60-75 mm   **Tails:** None

Description. Sexes differ: Male abdomen has white hairs, while female abdomen is black and shiny. Both sexes differ from *P. phoebus* (66) by having solid-black antennae. Sphragis of bred ♀ is keeled. Ground color of wings chalky white; no red or yellow circular spots on FW.

Habitat. Snowy mountains in n. part of range, but also in snowless Coast Range Mts. of n. Calif., where it flies in open patches of dry grass.

Flight. June and July in Washington; May and June in California.

Food Plants. Bleedingheart, *Dicentra formosa* and *D. uniflora*. *D. nevadensis* and *D. cucullaria* probable.

Early Stages. Larva black with yellow markings; the larva overwinters, and completes growth the following year. The pupa is enclosed in a silken cocoon, which is regarded as a primitive trait.

Distribution. This is the only strictly N.A. species of the genus. Southern Alaska to Vancouver Isl., S through both e. and w. Washington; E through Idaho and mts. of w. Montana. (Not in Colo.). In Oregon it is the predominant species. In Calif., down Sierra Nevada as far S as Yosemite, from 5000 to 10,000 ft. In Yosemite from Transition Life Zone to lower Hudsonian, usually flying over thickets rather than in open alpine fields. Down Calif. Coast Range to Santa Cruz Co.

Subspecies. *P. clodius: incredibilis*, Mt. Elias, Alaska; *pseudogallatinus*,

Mt. Rainier N to B.C.; *claudianus*, s. Oregon to B.C.; *clodius*, n. Coast Range, Calif.; *altaurus*, se. B.C. to ne. Oregon and w. Wyo.; *baldur*, Sierra Nevada, Calif., w. Wash., Jackson Hole, Wyo.; *shepardi*, Spalding, Idaho; *menetriesii*, ne. Utah; *gallatinus*, nw. Wyo. and w. Mont.; *sol*, mountains of n. Calif.; *strohbeeni*, Santa Cruz Co., Calif.

66. *Parnassius phoebus* (Fabricius) 1793 Pl. XVI, Figs. 3,4.

PHOEBUS PARNASSIAN (formerly called, *P. smintheus*)

Expanse: 55-75 mm **Tails:** None

Description. Sexes differ. Both sexes display white antennae with black rings, a contrast which is visible to the naked eye. Female UpFW has two red spots beyond apex of cell (also present in some ♂♂). Male is usually plainer than ♀. Spots may be yellow instead of red in either sex, or all black in ♂. Species extremely variable.

Habitat. Flies in openings of forest to the grassy fields above timberline in the mountains of Alaska and the West, reaching the highest peaks.

Flight. June through August.

Food Plants. Stonecrop (*Sedum lanceolatum* and *S. obtusatum*); western roseroot (*Rhodiola rosea*); all in family Crassulaceae. *Saxifraga* spp. (of Saxifragaceae).

Early Stages. Larva downy black with yellow spots on sides of each segment. Caterpillars feed through the summer and then go into hibernation in August, passing the winter in the next-to-last larval stage.

Distribution. In North America it flies in Alaska S of the Arctic Circle; n. Alberta, Canada, S to n. New Mexico; Utah; British Columbia, Canada, S to c. Sierra Nevada in California.

Subspecies. *P. phoebus behrii*, c. Sierra Nevada, Calif.; *sternitzkyi*, Siskiyou and Shasta Cos., Calif.; *olympianus*, Olympic Mts. and n. Cascades in Wash. and sw. B.C. (*gyppyi* may be included); *smintheus*, Canadian Rockies of Alberta and B.C. and s. B.C. except sw. and Vanc. Isl. (*nanus* and *magnus* may be included here); *xanthus*, intermediate and doubtful, from Idaho, e. and c. Wash., e. Ore. (*idahoensis* is a synonym); *montanulus*, Mont. and nw. Wyo. (includes *maximus*); *sayii*, e. Wyo., Black Hills of S.D., Colo.,

Utah, and e. Nevada (includes *dakotaensis, hollandi*, and *rubiana*); alt. f. "hermodur", is the high elevation form of *P. phoebus*, (includes *rotgeri*); *pseudorotgeri*, s. Colo. and n. N.M.

P. *phoebus apricatus*, Kodiak Is. Alaska; *golovinus*, w. and n. Alaska; *elias*, Mt. St. Elias and Skagway, Alaska; *alaskaensis*, Mt. McKinley Nat. Park, Alaska; *yukonensis*, Yukon Terr. and Atlin, B.C.

James Ebner has called my attention to specimens of *Parnassius* collected in Mexico which are now in the Milwaukee Public Museum. I should like to thank Dr. Allen M. Young, Head of the Divison of Invertebrate Zoology at the Museum, and Susan Borkin, Scientific Assistant, for supplying the following information. The specimens comprise two males and one female, collected by Arthur M. Moeck on 3 July 1952, at 350 m (1500) ft, in the vicinity of Victoria, Tamaulipas, Mexico. (These are labeled *Parnassius smintheus* Dbl. & Hew.) It is curious that this population of *P. phoebus* occurs in the Eastern Sierra Madre rather than in the Western division, since the nearest U.S. population would be the subspecies in the northern mountains of New Mexico.

I would also like to thank Kanelm W. Philip, Research Associate of the Institute of Arctic Biology, who has written to inform me that a population of *P. phoebus* has been discovered in the Arrigetch Peaks, near Walker Lake, which is north of the Arctic Circle. How extensive this intrusion into the Brooks Range of Alaska is, remains to be determined.

Note. For contemporary views on American *Parnassius* consult: section in W. H. Howe, *The Butterflies of North America*, 1975, pp. 403-409, by Jon H. and Sigrid Shepard. Clifford D. Ferris, "A Proposed Revision of Non-arctic *Parnassius phoebus* Fabricius in North America." *Jour. of Res. on Lepid.*, 1976. "A Note on the Subspecies of *Parnassius clodius* Ménétriés Found in the Rocky Mountains of the United States." (Same author and pub. data.) Also, John F. Emmel is revising the *P. clodius* complex (unpublished at this date).

III

A SURVIVOR

Subfamily BARONIINAE

While the single species in this subfamily looks something like a Parnassian in size and appearance, it is believed to be much more ancient, and is in fact a relict species. In Argentina there are two (other) relict species, and in Australia a third, but these belong to the Aristolochia-feeding True Swallowtails and would be more recent, even though very old. This Mexican species, with a subfamily all to itself, is much more ancient than any other member of the Swallowtail Family.

13

LIVING FOSSILS

Genus **Baronia**   Salvin 1893

If *Baronia brevicornis* had been discovered on the island of Komodo in Indonesia, along with the dragon lizard, in the heart of the presumed region of origin of the Swallowtail Family, there would have been less to puzzle over. However, its present geographical distribution is west and south from Mexico City and south of the transverse volcanic range, which provokes some interesting speculations. If the Papilionids were in fact the first family of true butterflies, this relict would represent the earliest surviving species of the superfamily to which all true butterflies belong. At the time when butterflies were beginning to differentiate, Mexico was not only separated from South America by a considerable body of water, but much of today's Mexico was also submerged, and the western Sierra Madre then existed only as a long peninsula integral with ancient North America (see Hoffmann 1933). Presumably *Baronia brevicornis* at that time inhabited the tip of this peninsula.

In addition to the enigma of place, the early stages of *B. brevicornis* were for a long time unknown, and that knowledge was essential in judging the place of so different a species. Because it had the fore-tibial epiphysis (spur) this insect was assumed to be a member of the Swallowtail Family, but unlike other members of the family it has both anal veins on the hind wing, like Pierids and Nymphalids. Hence it was necessary to assume that *brevicornis* diverged before the time when the

177

vein was lost by members of the Papilionid family. Then, in 1961, Vazquez and Perez published the first accounts of the life history. The larva does possess a forked scent organ (osmeterium) so *brevicornis* truly belongs in the family. On the other hand, the larval food plant confounded expectation by belonging to the Pea family, being an Acacia much like our desert catclaw.

67.   *Baronia brevicornis* Salvin 1893

SHORT-HORNED SWALLOWTAIL   Pl. XVI, Figs. 7,8.

Expanse: 55-65 mm   **Tails:** None.

Description. Sexes differ in some individuals. Antennae very short. HW rounded, as in Parnassians, but outer margin of FW comparatively straight. Wings brown or blackish brown, with yellow spotting. In some females the yellow spots run together, especially on HW, so that they become yellow butterflies with dark spots.

Habitat. Seemingly, thickets of deciduous scrub—"de selva baja caducifolia." The native name for the larval food plant is *cubata* and the thickets are called *cubatera*. Other plants in the growth are: *Bursera* spp., torchwood; *Ipomoea* spp., morning glory; *Mimosa polyantha*; *Neobuxbaumia mezcalaensis*; etc.

Flight. Records known to author run from May through August.

Food Plants. *Acacia cymbispina*. The food trees are bare until the first rains come, and as they leaf out the butterflies emerge. Adult females lay their eggs singly, a few on each tree. Said to be single-brooded.

Early Stages. Mature larva has a black or yellow head and a pea-green body with small tubercles which may be either black or yellow. Body has a continuous yellow dorsal stripe, and white transverse lines on each segment. The larvae are apparently able to dig themselves into the ground, or at least the rubble, for pupation.

Distribution. At localized points in the states of Guerrero, Morelos, Puebla, Michoacan, and Colima. Specific locales: kilometer 216 on railroad line from Mexico City to Acapulco, at 600 m (2000 ft). At Valerio Trujano, Guerrero, at 600 m (2000 ft). At Cañon de Lobos, Morelos, at 1200 m (4000 ft).

Forms. There are six named female forms, of which the most important are "eusemna" for the mostly yellow form, and "phronima" for the black.

GLOSSARY

Anal angle. Point at which inner margin of hind wing turns outward, away from abdomen; also called inner angle.

Anal eye spot. (See Fig. G.)

Anal vein(s). (See Fig. 2-1.)

Brood. Progeny of a given generation of adults.

Discal cell. (See Fig. G.)

Double-brooded. Producing two generations in one breeding season.

Expanse. Distance from one forewing tip to the other when wings are mounted at right angles to the body—as in the figures.

Flight. Period during which adults are flying.

Fringe spot. (See Fig. G.)

Lunate. Crescent-shaped (like the new moon).

Lunule. A small, crescent-shaped (lunate) spot.

Marginal band. (See Fig. G.)

Median band. A certain recognized arrangement of spots or areas of color having a more or less constant midwing locus but variable size. (See Fig. G.)

Pupil. A spot within a larger spot producing the semblance of an eye. (See Fig. G.)

Race. Geographical variant (subspecies).

Spatulate. Enlarged at one end, paddle-shaped.

Submarginal band. (See Fig. G.)

Subtropical. Used in this book as a translation of *templado-calida* of Hoffmann (1940b).

Typical form. That form which was the first one described.

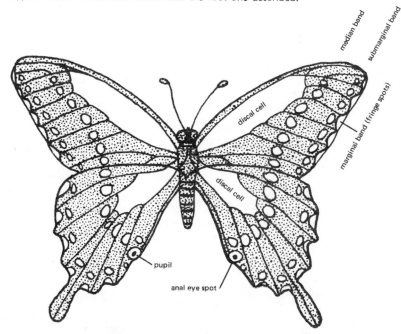

Figure G. Illustration of diagnostic terms.

SELECTED BIBLIOGRAPHY

LITERATURE CITED AND FURTHER READING

Bauer, D. L., 1955a, "Notes on the *Papilio machaon* Complex in Arizona," *The Lepidopterists' News* 9:7-10.

―――― 1955b, "A new race of *Papilio indra* from the Grand Canyon region," Ibid. 9:49-54.

Brower, J. V. Z., 1958, "Experimental Studies of Mimicry in some North American Butterflies, Pt. II. *Battus philenor* and *Papilio troilus, P. polyxenes* and *P. glaucus,*" *Evolution* 12:123-136.

Brower, L. P., 1958, "Larval Foodplant Specificity in Butterflies of the *Papilio glaucus* group," *The Lepidop. News* 12:103-114.

―――― 1959a, "Speciation in Butterflies of the *Papilio glaucus* Group. I. Morphological Relationships and Hybridization," *Evolution* 13:40-63.

―――― 1959b, "II. Ecological Relationships and Interspecific Behavior," Ibid. 13:213-228.

Brower, L. P., J. Alcock and J. V. Z. Brower, 1971, "Avian Feeding Behavior and the Selective Advantage of Incipient Mimicry," in R. Creed (ed.), *Ecological Genetics and Evolution,* 261-274. Oxford.

Clark, A. H., 1932a, "The Forms of the Common Old World Swallowtail Butterfly (*Papilio machaon*) in North America," *Proc. U.S. Nat. Mus.,* vol. 81, Art. 11. (Also see McDunnough 1934.)

Clarke, C. A., and P. M. Sheppard, 1955, "A Preliminary Report on the Genetics of the Machaon Group of Swt. Butterflies," *Evolution* 9:182-201.

―――― 1956, "A Further Report on the Genetics of the Machaon Group of Swallowtail Butterflies," Ibid. 10:66-73.

―――― 1957, "The breeding in captivity of the hybrid *Papilio glaucus* female X *Papilio eurymedon* male." *The Lepidop. News* 11:201-205.

Covell, C. V. C., and G. W. Rawson, 1973, "Project Ponceanus: A Report on First Efforts to Survey and Preserve the Schaus' Swt. in Southern Florida," *J. Lepid. Soc.* 27:206-209.

D'Almeida, R. F., 1966, *Catalogo dos Papilionidae Americanos,* Soc. Bras. de Ento., Sao Paulo.

Dethier, V. G., 1941, "Chemical factors determining the choice of food plants by *Papilio* larvae," *Amer. Nat.* 75:61-73.

dos Passos, C. F., 1964, *A Synonymic List of the Nearctic Rhopalocera,* The Lepid. Soc., Memoirs I.

Eff, D., 1962, "A little about the little-known *Papilio indra minori,*" *J. Lepid. Soc.* 16:137-142.

Ehrlich, P. R., and P. H. Raven, 1965, "Butterflies and Plants: a study in co-evolution," *Evolution* 18:586-608.

Elwes, H. J., 1886, "On Butterflies of the Genus *Parnassius,*" *Proc. Zool. Soc. Lond.* 6-53.

Emmel, J. F., and T. Emmel, 1967, "The Biology of *Papilio indra kaibabensis* in the Grand Canyon," *J. Lepid. Soc.* 21:41-48.

Ferguson, D., 1950, "Collecting a Little-known *PAPILIO,*" *The Lepid. News* 4:11-12.

Ford, E. B., 1944, "Studies on the Chemistry of Pigments in the Lepidoptera. . . . 4. The Classification of the Papilionidae," *Trans. R. Ent. Soc. Lond.* 94, Part 2.

Jordan, K., "Family I: Papilionidae, Swallowtails," in A. Seitz, *Macrolepidoptera of the Earth,* Vol. 5, 1907-08, pp. 11-51.

Levin, M. P., 1973, "Preferential mating and maintenance of the sex-limited dimorphism in *Papilio glaucus;* evidence from laboratory matings." *Evolution* 27:257-264.

McDunnough, J. H., 1934, "Notes on Canadian Diurnal Lepidoptera," *Canad. Ent.* 66:83-86.

Munroe, E. 1961, "The Classification of the Papilionidae (Lepidoptera), *Canad. Ent., Supplement* 17.

Munroe, E., and P. Ehrlich, 1960, "Harmonization of concepts of higher classification of the Papilionidae," *J. Lepid. Soc.* 14:169-175.

Newcomer, E. J., 1964, "Life histories of *Papilio indra* and *P. oregonius,*" *J. Res. on the Lepid.* 3:49-54.

Perkins, S. F., E. M. Perkins, Jr., and S. Shininger, 1968, "Ill. Life Hist. and Notes on *Papilio oregonius,*" *J. Lepid. Soc.* 22:53-56.

Remington, C. L., 1968, "A New Sibling *Papilio* from the Rocky Mountains, with Genetic and Biological Notes," *Postilla,* No. 119, New Haven.

Rothschild, W., and K. Jordan, 1906, "A Revision of the American Papilios," *Novitates Zoologicae* XIII, Reprint ed., San Francisco, 1967.

Rutkowski, F., 1971, "Observations on *Papilio aristodemus ponceanus,*" *J. Lepid. Soc.* 25:126-136

Saunders, A. A., 1932, *Butterflies of the Allegany State Park,* U. of State of N.Y., Albany.

Scriber, J. M., 1973, "Latitudinal Gradients in Larval Feeding Specialization of the World Papilionidae," *Psyche* 80:355-373, and *A Supplementary Table of Data.*

Shapiro, A. M., 1966, *Butterflies of the Delaware Valley,* Am. Ent. Soc., Philadelphia.

———— 1975, *"Papilio 'gothica'* and the phenotypic plasticity of *P. zelicaon,*" *J. Lepid. Soc.* 29:No. 2, 79-84.

Shields, O., 1967, "Hilltopping: An Ecological Study of Summit Congregation Behavior of Butterflies on a Southern Calif. Hill." *J. Res. on Lepid.* 6:69-178.

Slansky, F., Jr., 1972, "Latitudinal Gradients in Species Diversity of the New World Swallowtail Butterflies," Ibid., 11:201-217.

Wielgus, R. S., 1969, "The rearing of *Papilio indra kaibabensis,*" *J. Res. on Lepid.* 8:177-181.

Wilson, K. H., "Fam. Papilionidae," in P. R. Ehrlich and A. H. Ehrlich, *How to Know the Butterflies,* Dubuque, Ia. 1961, pp. 30-50.

Young, A. M., 1971, "Mimetic Associations in Natural Populations of Tropical Papilionid Butterflies," *J. of N.Y. Ent. Soc.* 79:210-224.

OF MEXICAN RELEVANCE

Brown, F. M., 1943, "Notes on Mexican Butterflies. I. Papilionidae," *J. N.Y. Ent. Soc.* 51:161-178.

Comstock, J., and L. Vazquez, 1960, "Estudios de los Ciclos Biologicos en Lepidopteros Mexicanos," *An. Inst. Biol. Mex.* 31:339-348.

Diaz Frances, Alberto, 1975, "Papilionidos del Valle de Tepoztlan, Morelos," *Boletin Informativo,* Sociedad Mexicana de Lepidopterologia, A.C.,1, No. 3, 5-7.

Gibson, W. W., and J. L. Carillo, 1959, "Lista de insectos en la collection entomologica de la Oficina de Estudios Especiales," S. A. G. *Folleto misc.,* No. 9., Mexico.

Godman, F. D., and O. Salvin, 1887-1901, *Biologia Centrali-Americana: Insecta: Lepid.-Rhop.* Vols. 1,2,3.

Graham, A. (ed.), 1973, *Vegetation and Vegetational History of Northern Latin America,* N.Y., American Elsevier Pub. Co.

Hoffmann, C. C., 1933, "La Fauna de Lepidopteros del distrito de Soconusco (Chiapas)," *An. Inst. Biol. Mex.* IV:207-225.
—— 1940a., "Lepid. Nuevos de Mexico V," Ibid. XI:634-635.
—— 1940b., "Catalogo de Lepidopteros Mexicanos," Ibid. XI:648ff.
—— 1940c., "*Papilio photinus* forma fem., ESCALANTEI, nov.," Ibid. XI:275.
Holland, R., 1972, "Butterflies of middle and southern Baja Calif.," *J. Res. on Lepid.* 11:147-160.
Leopold, A. S., 1959, "The Mexican Landscape," in, *Wildlife of Mexico, The Game Birds and Mammals,* U. of Calif. Press, Berkeley.
Powell, J. A., 1958, "Additions to the knowledge of the butterfly fauna of Baja California Norte," *Lepid. Soc. News* 12:26-32.
Racheli, T., and V. Sbordoni, 1975, "A New Species of *Papilio* from Mexico," *Fragmenta Entomologica,* Vol. XI, fasc. 2, 175-183.
Rindge, F. H., 1948, "Contributions toward a knowledge of the insect fauna of Lower Calif., No. 8, Lepid. Rhop." *Proc. Calif. Acad. of Sci.* 24:289-311.
Ross, G., 1964a., "Life History Studies on Mexican Butterflies. I," *J. Res. on Lepid.* 3:9-17.
—— 1964b., Ibid., III, 3:209-229.
—— 1967. A Distributional Study of the Butterflies of the Sierra de Tuxtla in Veracruz. A dissertation (#67-14,010) available from University Microfilms, Ann Arbor, Mich.
Schaus, W. J., 1883, "Early Stages of Some Mexican Lepid.," *Papilio* 3:186-189.
—— 1884, "Early Stages of Mexican Lepid.," Ibid. 4:100-103.
Serrano, F., and M. E. Serrano, 1972, *Las Mariposas de El Salvador, Primera Parte: Papilionidae,* Universidad de El Salvador.
Vazquez, L., 1947, "Papilios Nuevos de Mexico, I," *An. Inst. Biol. Mex.* 18:249-256.
—— 1948, Ibid., II, 19:233-240.
—— 1953, "Observaciones sobre Papilios de Mexico, con descriptiones de algunas formas nuevas; una especie nueva para Mexico y localidades nuevas de algunos otros, III," Ibid., 24:170-175.
—— 1956, "Papilios Nuevos de Mexico, IV," Ibid. 27:473-485.
Vazquez, L. and H. Perez, 1961, "Observaciones sobre la biologia de *Baronia brevicornis* Salv.," Ibid. 32:295-311.
—— 1967, "Nuevas observaciones sobre la biologia de *Baronia brevicornis,*" Ibid., 37:195-204.
Young, A. M., 1973, "Notes on the life cycle and natural history of *Parides arcas mylotes.* . . . in Costa Rican premontane wet forest," *Psyche* 80:1-21.

STATE AND PROVINCE BUTTERFLY BOOKS AND LISTS

B.C., Jones, J. R., 1951, "An Annotated Check-list of the Macrolepidoptera of British Columbia," Ent. Soc. B.C., *Occasional Papers* 1:1-140.
CA, Comstock, J. A., 1927, *Butterflies of California,* Los Angeles.
CA, Emmel, T. C., and J. F. Emmel, 1973, *The Butterflies of Southern California,* Nat. Hist. Mus. of Los Angeles Co.
CO, Brown, F. M., 1957, *Colorado Butterflies,* Denver Mus. Nat. Hist.
DC, Clark, A. H., 1932b, *The Butterflies of the District of Columbia and Vicinity,* U.S. Nat. Mus. Bull. 157.
FL, Kimball, C. P. 1965, *The Lepidoptera of Florida,* Division of Plant Industry, Gainsville.
GA, Harris, L., 1972, *Butterflies of Georgia,* U. of Oklahoma Press, Norman.

IL, Irwin, R. R., and J. C. Downey, 1973, *Annotated Checklist of the Butterflies of Illinois,* Ill. Nat. Hist. Survey, Urbana.

IN, Shull, E. M., and F. S. Badger, 1972, "Annotated List of Butterflies of Indiana," *J. Lepid Soc.* 26:13-24.

KS, Field, W. D., 1940, *A Manual of the Butterflies and Skippers of Kansas,* U. of Kansas, Bull. 39.

KY, Covell, C. V., Jr., 1974, "A Preliminary Checklist of the Butterflies of Kentucky," *J. Lepid. Soc.* 28:253-256.

LA, Lambremont, E. N., 1954, "The Butterflies and Skippers of Louisiana," *Tulane Studies in Zool.* 1:127-164.

ME, Brower, A. E., 1974, *List of the Lepidoptera of Maine—Part 1, The Macrolepidoptera,* Orono, Maine.

MD, Fales, John H. 1974, "Checklist of the Skippers and Butterflies of Maryland," *Chesapeake Science,* 15:222-229.

MI, Moore, S., 1960, "A Revised Annotated List of the Butterflies of Michigan," *Occas. Papers, Mus. Zool.,* U. of Mich.

MN, Huber, R. L., et al., 1966, *A Systematic Checklist of Minnesota Rhopalocera,* The Science Museum, St. Paul.

MS, Mather, B., and K. Mather, 1958, "The Butterflies of Mississippi," *Tulane Studies in Zool.,* 6:63-109.

MT, Elrod, M. J., 1906, *The Butterflies of Montana,* U. Mont. Bull. 30.

NB, Johnson, K., 1973, "The Butterflies of Nebraska," *J. Res. on Lepid.* 11:1-64.

NM, Holland, R., 1972, "Butterflies of Six Central New Mexico Mountains. . . .", *J. Lepid. Soc.* 28:38-52.

NY, Shapiro, A. M., 1974, "Butterflies and Skippers of New York State," *Search,* Vol. 4, No. 3, Ithaca, N.Y.

NC, Brimley, C. S., 1938, "Lepidoptera," *The Insects of North Carolina,* pp. 255-313, Div. of Ent., N.C. Dept. of Ag., Raleigh.

ND, Puckering, D. L., and R. L. Post, 1960, *The Butterflies of North Dakota,* N.D. Ag. College, Publ. 1, Fargo.

Nova Scotia, Ferguson, D. C., 1955, "The Lepidoptera of Nova Scotia, Pt. I," *Nova Scotia Mus. of Sci. Bull.* 2:161-375.

Ont., Riotte, J. C., 1971, "Butterflies and Skippers of Northern Ontario," *Mid-Continent Lepid. Series* 2(21):1-20.

OR, Anon., 1972, "Check List of Oregon Rhopalocera," Ibid., 4(57):1-11.

PA, Tietz, H. M., 1952, *The Lepidoptera of Pennsylvania, A Manual,* Penn. State Coll. of Ag., University Park.

Sask., Hooper, R. H., 1973, *Butterflies of Saskatchewan,* Sask. Dept. of Nat. Resources, Regina.

TX, Kendall, R. O., 1963, *The Butterflies and Skippers of Texas, A Tentative List,* Welder Wildlife Foundation, Sinton.

UT, Tidwell, K. B., and C. J. Callaghan, 1972, "A Checklist of Utah Butterflies and Skippers," *Mid-Cont. Lepid. Ser.* 4(57):1-16.

VA, Clark, A. H. and E. F. Clark, 1951, *The Butterflies of Virginia,* Smithsonian Misc. Colls., 116, Wash. D. C.

WA, Leighton, B. B., 1946, "The Butterflies of Washington," *Mid-Con. Lepid. Ser.* 4(54):1-15.

WA, Pyle, R. M., 1974, *Watching Washington Butterflies,* Seattle Audubon Society.

WI, Ebner, J. A., 1970, *Butterflies of Wisconsin,* Milwaukee Public Mus., Pop. Sci. Handbook No. 12.

WY, Ferris, C. D., 1971, *An Annotated Checklist of the Rhopalocera [Butterflies] of Wyoming,* U. of Wyo. Sci. Monograph 23, Laramie.

INDEX OF SWALLOWTAIL NAMES

184

INDEX OF LARVAL FOOD PLANTS

GENERAL INDEX
(place names not indexed)